The Noisy Classroom

Debate and critical oracy allow students to deepen their knowledge and understanding of academic subjects while simultaneously developing their communication and critical thinking skills, which can be hugely effective in increasing attainment. This book, written by an experienced teacher and founder of The Noisy Classroom, aims to help students learn to argue, disagree and debate in a constructive manner. Packed with resources and engaging exercises, it shows teachers how to develop an argument culture in the classroom that promotes open-mindedness and encourages students to explore new perspectives, defend views and challenge others.

The Noisy Classroom includes:

- A reflection on critical oracy and why it is important.

- A step-by-step guide for teachers to set up and encourage debate across the curriculum, highlighting how to get the most out of a noisy classroom.

- Advice for teachers on how to overcome barriers to building and using critical oracy in the classroom, including troubleshooting when things go wrong.

- Practical ideas for sharpening pair, group and whole-class discussions, ranging from small starter and plenary activities to full parliamentary-style debates.

The book brings together activities gathered and tested over 20 years of working in debate, oracy and education. It is intended for school teachers, including both NQTs and more experienced practitioners.

Debbie Newman has been involved in oracy education for 18 years, firstly as the Head of the Centre for Speech and Debate at the English-Speaking Union and then as a secondary English teacher and whole-school lead on the spoken word. She was the coach of the England Schools Debating Team from 2006 to 2009, winning the World Schools Debating Championships in 2008. Debbie founded and developed The Noisy Classroom, an organisation that trains teachers, produces resources and runs workshops and programmes for students in debate and critical oracy.

The Noisy Classroom

Developing Debate and Critical Oracy in Schools

Debbie Newman

Routledge
Taylor & Francis Group

LONDON AND NEW YORK

First published 2020
by Routledge
2 Park Square, Milton Park, Abingdon, Oxon OX14 4RN

and by Routledge
52 Vanderbilt Avenue, New York, NY 10017

Routledge is an imprint of the Taylor & Francis Group, an informa business

British Library Cataloguing-in-Publication Data
A catalogue record for this book is available from the British Library

Library of Congress Cataloging-in-Publication Data
Names: Newman, Debbie, author.
Title: The noisy classroom : developing debate and critical oracy in
    schools / Debbie Newman.
Description: Abingdon, Oxon ; New York, NY : Routledge, 2020.
Identifiers: LCCN 2019020965 (print) | LCCN 2019980957 (ebook) | ISBN
    9781138496910 (hardback) | ISBN 9781138496927 (paperback) | ISBN
    9781351020220 (ebook)
Subjects: LCSH: Oral communication—Study and teaching. | Critical
    thinking—Study and teaching. | Debates and debating—Study and
    teaching. | Student-centered learning.
Classification: LCC P95.3 .N49 2019 (print) | LCC P95.3 (ebook) | DDC
    370.11/5—dc23
LC record available at https://lccn.loc.gov/2019020965
LC ebook record available at https://lccn.loc.gov/2019980957

ISBN: 978-1-138-49691-0 (hbk)
ISBN: 978-1-138-49692-7 (pbk)
ISBN: 978-1-351-02022-0 (ebk)

Typeset in Melior
by Cenveo® Publisher Services

For Charles Dormer, the teacher who got me started on this journey.

Contents

Foreword

Brian Lightman

At a time when so many aspects of our education system are measured and judged in relation to outcomes from written tasks and examinations, it would be easy to understate the importance of oracy skills. Yet the impact these skills have on academic attainment is underpinned by ample research evidence. Most importantly, they are an essential life skill. Ask any employer about the skills and attributes they value in young people, and the ability to communicate orally will be high on their priority list.

Yet the development of these skills needs to be an integral and carefully planned part of the curriculum. Every teacher needs to understand the pedagogical tools that can be used to develop and teach these skills. The distinction between what the author describes as "performance oracy" and "critical oracy", and the strong case for development of the latter, is very important and thought-provoking.

Debbie Newman is an expert on these matters. This book provides a wealth of insight into this topic in three ways:

- First, it sets out with great clarity the case for critical oracy with the reasons why such skills are important.

- Second, it analyses the potential barriers, perceived or actual, that can hold some schools back from raising the profile of these skills.

- Third, it provides a veritable Aladdin's cave of techniques and tools to develop these skills with a host of suggested techniques for teachers to use.

From a personal perspective as a former teacher of modern languages, I find that many of these techniques resonate strongly with my most successful teaching, but, more importantly, they reflect some of the most inspiring and fulfilling aspects of my teaching and school leadership experience. My classrooms often were "noisy" in a purposeful and educational sense! Sometimes teachers (particularly those with less experience) are fearful that these activities will lead to poor behaviour and noise of the wrong kind. Where expectations are clear and relationships right, my experience is that this fear is unfounded.

Time and again, I have seen how the development of oracy skills embeds students' understanding in a powerful way. The provision of opportunities for students to play an active part in the development of their school through activities that give them a true voice about important and relevant matters greatly strengthens a school ethos. Conversely, valuable learning opportunities are missed when these techniques are not used.

As an education consultant and former school inspector, I have seen on multiple occasions the way in which the lessons that require students to articulate and explain what they have been taught give them access to truly deep learning. Developing this into critical oracy enables young people to engage in subject matter at a depth that is frequently not accessed.

That experience also extends well beyond the formal classroom. Opportunities to present in front of different audiences, to engage in student voice activities and to participate in debating give access to a rich experience. Involvement in such activities enables students to engage intelligently in discussion about topical and often controversial issues, to grow cultural capital and to become active citizens within and beyond their schools. And, of course, as Debbie eloquently explains, they provide powerful preparation for students' future working lives and study at higher levels.

I commend this book to all teachers. I have no doubt that using the approaches the book describes will not only improve academic outcomes but also significantly add to the richness of the education provided.

Acknowledgements

Many thanks to Charles Barnett, Sarah Spikesley, Iain Lynn and students from Redden Court School and Clapton Girls' Academy for contributing to this book. Special thanks to Ian Howes, Jon Evans and especially Chris Wolsey for contributing to the book and also for reading drafts and offering their ideas and suggestions. Thanks to all the students who allowed me to hone my skills at teaching debate and critical oracy, especially those who took part in programmes run by the English-Speaking Union, the PiXL Club and the Linklaters' Hackney Debating programme and at Westcliff High School for Boys. Thanks to my colleagues Alice Coombes Huntley and Harold Raitt for developing ideas alongside me. Finally, thanks to the anonymous originators of many of the exercises in this book who have made such a positive contribution to classroom practice.

Part I

The case for critical oracy

Introduction

I want your students to argue with you more. And not just with you but also with each other, with great thinkers of the past and with today's leaders. I want them to argue, and I want them to argue well. I want to them to be critical thinkers; careful, active listeners; and persuasive speakers. The education I have in mind in my vision of a noisy classroom is one where students question and interrogate everything that is put before them. They listen with an open mind, are willing to consider all perspectives and are not afraid to defend their views and challenge others or to change their mind if they find themselves convinced. Of course, in so doing, they will find themselves in the long and fine tradition of academia over millennia. One seldom moves forward without understanding the body of knowledge that came before. Progress comes by questioning that knowledge. Plato challenged Aristotle, Einstein challenged Newton, and Friedman challenged Keynes. To do the same, students need the opportunity to engage in debate and critical oracy. Certainly, argument happens in writing too, but it is slow. You must wait until someone has read your work and responded to it in their own work before you can offer a counter-rebuttal. This might be possible for university fellows, but it is less practical for your Year 10 English class. Most school pupils' experience of argument will primarily be through the spoken word, and whole-class, group and pair activities can be designed to allow disagreement to flourish constructively. When pupils have to put forward their own written argument and show an understanding of multiple perspectives in their examinations, they will, of course, be admirably prepared.

By its nature, debating can seem very adversarial. It need not be, however, and not all of the exercises in this book are combative. That said, they all require students to engage critically with each other and their studies. The activities contained within this book will help them to develop their thinking and their communication skills and prepare them for university, the workplace and civic life.

Who is this book for?

This book is aimed primarily at secondary school teachers who wish to embed more debate and critical oracy into their lessons. It is suitable for teachers of all disciplines, studying any curriculum and teaching any age from 11 to 18. It is also useful for senior managers or literacy leads who wish to introduce more debate and oracy across their school. Teachers of English as an additional language (EAL), or indeed any foreign language, will find the activities a useful and engaging way of practising speaking and listening skills. Adults involved in running youth groups will also find many exercises that would be appropriate for their context.

How can I use this book?

Part I of the book looks at the case for more debate and critical oracy in schools. It covers what critical oracy is, why teachers should be doing more of it and how to overcome the barriers to doing more. It also looks at some of the overarching issues of running oracy-based activities, discussing the role of senior managers and teachers, troubleshooting and assessment.

Part II of the book is a toolkit for oracy-based activities that teachers of all subjects can use to introduce more high-quality, structured talk into their classrooms. Teachers should dip into these activities in any order, and there is no need to read Part I first if you already run oracy-based activities and are looking for more ideas to broaden your practice or if just want to get started.

This part starts with set-piece debating, the jewel in the crown of critical oracy. It then goes on to cover other debate formats, shorter activities that are perfect for starters and plenaries, in-character activities such as Hot Seating and Mock Trials that are terrific for helping students to see different perspectives and structured activities to replace more free-form whole-class, group and pair discussion. The last chapter looks at some ideas for activities that explicitly develop oracy skills, rather than using oracy to deliver the rest of the curriculum. Each of these activities includes instructions for running the activity, possible topics covering a variety of disciplines, planning and resources needed and any other points to consider.

In the appendices, you'll find some detailed resources such as speech scaffolding sheets and assessment criteria for debates, key vocabulary for debate and ideas for sentences stems, connectives and debate and discussion topics.

How did this book come about?

This book brings together activities gathered and tested over 20 years of working in debate, oracy and education. At the start of my career, I was fortunate enough to work at the Centre for Speech and Debate at the English-Speaking Union (ESU), where I felt myself so lucky to take that often-wished-for path of turning my hobby into my job. I had loved the thrill of debating ever since I took part in my first inter-form debate when I was 11 years old. Debating had become a passion as I competed nationally and internationally through school and university, and it was at Cambridge that I was afforded opportunities to teach debate too. And so my intentions to enrol in a law-conversion course diminished, and I found myself heading to Dartmouth House, the glorious headquarters of the ESU. It was an exciting time to be at the ESU. Under the direction of Marc Whitmore, the Centre for Speech and Debate was widening its focus from competitive debate to debate outreach and debate in the curriculum. I had opportunities to learn so much from colleagues at the ESU, the International Debate Academy in Slovenia, the World Schools Debating Championships and especially at the World Debate Institute in Vermont, then under the leadership of the late and incomparable Professor Alfred "Tuna" Snider. There are so many professional and amateur debate trainers of great skill and passion, and it is extremely rewarding to be a part of this community.

I learnt just as much when I left the ESU to become an English teacher. I was lucky to work in a school, and a department, with an established culture of oracy, and there I discovered the power of debate and critical discussion in a new way. I experienced first-hand the power that lies in debate's ability to deepen understanding and help pupils to appreciate multiple perspectives. I saw close up its value in securing unprecedented levels of student engagement. I experienced the magic of a silent classroom in which 30 students were working next each other writing and reading, and I also experienced the magic of a noisy classroom in which 30 students in pairs were simultaneously arguing over a text in a vibrant, exciting forum. I am convinced that both forms of learning should be part of students' day-to-day education. Some pupils will naturally excel more than others, but all students must have the opportunity to improve at both. Debating and critical oracy are not just for the most gifted and enthusiastic; they are for everyone.

Over the last ten years, The Noisy Classroom has been working with schools, building the skills and confidence their teachers need to incorporate debate and critical oracy into their classroom practice and running workshops directly for pupils. During this time, I have learnt so much from teachers about how activities can be adapted and applied to different curriculum areas. There's nothing better than receiving positive feedback from a maths or physical education (PE) teacher about an oracy-based lesson that they have run! If something works for you—a particular topic, unit or activity—I would love to hear from you at debbie@noisyclassroom.com.

I hope you find a lot of joy running the activities in this book and seeing all the ways in which your students may surprise you.

What is critical oracy, and what is the state of oracy in our schools at the moment?

What is critical oracy?

"Oracy" is the currently favoured term for what at other times has been called "speaking and listening" or "the spoken word". Although no term is perfect, oracy has the advantage of suggesting parity with literacy and numeracy. It covers all verbal communication skills from presenting to questioning, summarising to storytelling, listening to negotiating. It covers the formal and the informal and encompasses everything from a one-on-one conversation to an address delivered to the nation.

It is important to make the distinction between "performance oracy" and "critical oracy". Performance oracy includes reading aloud, reciting poetry and learning and performing the lines of a play—and perhaps telling stories and delivering a memorized speech. Performance oracy can be an excellent tool for building confidence, developing memory and building empathy. It is valuable in and of itself without necessarily contributing to students' further learning across the curriculum. Very often, there is a limited amount of time that teachers outside of English and drama faculties would feel they could give to these formats.

Critical oracy is talk that involves engaging with other people, ideas and the outside world and includes discussion, debate, advocacy, enquiry and role play. When a class is involved in critical oracy, speaking and thinking (or listening and thinking) are happening simultaneously. Critical oracy is different from performance oracy, as it is a way of engaging with core learning. Having absorbed a literary text, a historical source or new scientific knowledge, the students then argue with the teacher, each other and scholars from across the ages about the interpretation and application of that knowledge. That is why the progressive v traditional, skills v knowledge tussle has no place here. When students are debating whether the Treaty of Versailles led to World War II, are you in a progressive or a traditional classroom? They are using critical thinking and communication skills to fully understand the knowledge with which they are being presented. They are questioning, clarifying, challenging, interrogating, defending and summarising the curriculum. Critical oracy prepares us for examinations, interviews, civic discourse and workplace communication in a way that performance oracy does not, and it is the concern of this book.

What is the state of oracy in our schools at the moment?

As with everything in education, the picture of oracy varies greatly from school to school. In some schools, teachers report that as much as they would love to debate in the classroom, it is forbidden by leadership teams that want traditional teaching, all work in books and silent classrooms. In other schools, oracy is embraced from top to bottom with oracy lead teachers, assessment criteria and whole-school projects and training. Other schools may have quite a lot of talk in the classroom but without the planning and structures to get the most out of it. On a national level, the profile of oracy has been boosted by School 21, an all-through comprehensive school in East London. Oracy is integral to teaching and learning at the school, and it is taught explicitly through the Oracy Framework, co-created with Oracy Cambridge, University of Cambridge. The success of the approach led to the establishment of two Education Endowment Foundation pilots assessing the applicability of oracy across the curriculum and in schools across the UK and to the founding of Voice 21, a charity dedicated to raising the status of oracy in UK schools with a focus on teacher professional development. Along with the English-Speaking Union (ESU), which has renewed its focus on oracy in the classroom, Voice 21 has developed the Oracy Network and supported the launch of an All Party Parliamentary Group on Oracy.

In 2017, Voice 21 commissioned a report titled *Oracy: The State of Speaking in Our Schools*, and its findings give a useful snapshot of the national picture. For example:

- 68% teachers agree that is it "very important I develop my pupils' oracy skills".

- 57% of teachers say that they have had no training in oracy over the past three years.

- 20% of schools formally communicate with parents about the quality of pupils' verbal contributions.

- 16% of schools have a school-wide policy for oracy.[1]

Oracy took a blow when marks for speaking and listening were removed from the English Language General Certificate of Secondary Education (GCSE) in 2014, disincentivising a focus on building these skills. With no oracy feeding directly into examination results and with no accountability through Ofsted, schools can, and sometimes do, feel able to neglect this area. Some schools, however, see this freedom as an opportunity to use initiative and imagination in their teaching, without feeling they are being made a slave to data or compelled to go through a tick-box exercise.

Note

1 Millard, W., and Menzies, L. (2016) *Oracy: The State of Speaking in Our Schools.* London: LKMco and Voice 21.

2 Why is critical oracy important?

What skills are developed through debate and critical oracy?

A mixture of qualitative and quantitative research over the years has found that the following skills can be developed through formal debating:

Structured thought
Analysis/reasoning
Critical listening
Use of evidence
Self-confidence
Persuasive speaking skills
Teamwork
Research
Thinking on your feet, under pressure
Ability to see two sides of an issue
Ability to argue in a constructive, non-personal way
Ability to detect bias
Use of formal vocabulary
Use of standard English

Teachers also report that students find debating fun, and it can engage them further with their learning and develop greater understanding of subject matter.

Not all of these skills are equally developed through activities beyond Parliamentary and Table Debates, but all of the activities in this book develop at least some of these skills. Other activities may build additional skills; for example, the in-character tasks lend themselves to building empathy.

Participating in debate and critical oracy and developing these skills can lead to advantages in many areas of education and wider society.

Academic understanding and achievement

Taking part in critical oracy activities builds students' critical thinking skills and allows them to explore a subject in depth, interrogate knowledge and build understanding.

A number of studies have linked debating to increased academic attainment:

■ Researchers found that Chicago students who participate in academic debate programs are twice as likely to attain the ACT college-readiness benchmark in English and 70% more likely to attain the ACT college-readiness benchmark in reading as comparable peers who did not participate in academic debate in high school.[1]

■ The Centre for British Teachers (CFBT) report commissioned by the ESU found evidence for debating leading to improved attainment in biology, art, history, reading and critical thinking and cited research in the USA conducted by the Urban Debate League showing that debaters in urban high schools were 25% more likely to complete school than non-debaters.[2]

More research needs to be conducted in the UK, but these mainly American findings chime with the qualitative feedback given by teachers and also our intuitive understanding of the benefits of debate. Other studies show the benefits of wider oracy activities:

■ The Education Endowment Foundation has reviewed the evidence for collaborative learning, saying that "Over 40 years a number of systematic reviews and meta-analyses have provided consistent evidence about the benefits of collaborative learning" and emphasising that "approaches which promote talk and interaction between learners tend to result in the best gains".[3]

There are many ways in which an oracy-rich classroom can help attainment.

Talk before writing

Pupils model thought and language before they put pen to paper, and they benefit from discussing ideas before they try to write about them. Collaborative reasoning helps us to make sense of complicated problems and situations—human brains evolved for collaboration.

Talk for assessment

Writing is less immediate than talk, and the feedback loop is delayed to the point of being disrupted. A faulty premise can be picked up immediately in dialogue so that a whole piece of work does not go on to be based upon it. Speaking is the most time-efficient way to give formative feedback, and it is the type of assessment for learning that allows a teacher to modify the difficulty, direction or scope of the lesson as it unfolds.

Talk to share and refine ideas

Conversation allows for the sharing of ideas through peers, and critical oracy allows thought to be refined through challenge and defence. In English literature, for example, if an interpretation of a text is challenged, then the student must find the best evidence from the text to back up their argument. In history, students' analytical skills must be honed to show why one cause is more likely than another. In science, students must learn how to clearly articulate the effects of a scientific development on the community.

Talk to build essay and examination skills

Formal debating and its related activities are especially effective for preparing students for examinations, as they grow the skills of quickly thinking on their feet under pressure. Debating has the added benefit of being extremely structured. Pupils learn how to develop an extended response that is broken down into points, each of which is analysed and supported by evidence. This has knock-on benefits for essay writing and examination technique.

Talk to build higher-order thinking skills

Effective speaking enables teachers to move away from the lower tiers of Bloom's Taxonomy to challenge students in higher-order thinking. Most of the activities in this book require students to take part in the application, analysis, synthesis and/or evaluation of knowledge. The language needed to engage in these activities and hone these skills can be modelled, shared, scaffolded and supported to help all students refine their thinking abilities.

Talk to build vocabulary

Having academic vocabulary used regularly in classroom talk could also help academic achievement. Alex Quigley has written on the impact that the vocabulary gap has on the wider achievement gap. He points to the fact that the language gap at age three correlates to the later gaps in reading and mathematics. One of his suggestions for closing the gap (alongside, among others, explicitly teaching vocabulary and strategies for reading and writing) is to "promote and scaffold high quality academic talk in the classroom".[4] In addition, for EAL students, and for all students in a foreign language classroom, significant amounts of high-quality talk can help to embed a wider vocabulary and have an impact on writing too.

Skills for the workplace

Time and time again we hear from businesses that they need their employees to have better communication skills. A 2014 report by the British Chamber of Commerce, which surveyed over 3,000 firms, found that 57% of respondents thought young people lacked the basic soft skills of communication and teamwork.[5] The 2016 CBI/Pearson Education and Skills Survey found that 50% of businesses were not satisfied with the communication skills of school and college leavers.[6] Working in teams, interacting with clients and customers, selling, managing, resolving conflict, pitching, presenting and participating in many other parts of day-to-day working life involve communication. With an increasing focus on a post-automation workforce, communication only becomes more important in the toolbox of employability skills. A current focus on "21st century skills" often includes critical thinking, collaboration and communication,[7] all of which we develop through debate. Of course, these skills are not new and have been seen in curricula going back millennia, but they are receiving particular attention in today's workplace.

There is then the fact that to get a job in the first place, one must usually have an oral interview, so lack of verbal communication skills can form a barrier to employment from the start. Furthermore, Project Oxygen, Google's effort to determine what qualities are important in their top employees, lists "communicating and listening well" alongside "possessing insights into others (including others' different values and points of views)" and "being a good critical thinker and problem solver".[8] These skills are especially linked to debating and oracy activities, which encourage the airing of different views.

Preparation for university

The confidence and skill needed to express oneself verbally are crucial to thriving at university in many subjects. Seminar teaching expects the ability to articulate your thoughts within a wider academic dialogue. Critically engaging with material, assessing evidence and comparing different interpretations and approaches are at the heart of much of the study of the humanities, arts and social sciences. If a student's prior experience of this is limited to having been drilled in including one paragraph in their essays in which they say, "Some people may argue x; however…", as an exercise in ticking a box for an examiner, they are ill-prepared for the rigour of higher-level academic practice. If from Year Seven onwards (and in fact earlier), they have been exposed to a culture of critical oracy in which ideas are aired, built on, interrogated, supported and challenged, there will be no "shock". They will be critical thinkers and curious learners prepared to challenge and be challenged in a thoughtful and reasoned way. Of the four sets of skills that are needed to thrive that are highlighted by the University of Cambridge, three can be developed through debate and critical oracy: intellectual skills, communication skills and interpersonal skills.[9]

Of all home students in the UK starting full-time degree courses for the first time in 2015-16, more than one in ten were expected to leave higher education without a qualification.[10] Research in the USA shows that debating and discussion in the curriculum can lead to higher college matriculation and retention among at-risk students.[11] Could we see similar effects with a debate-led curriculum in the UK?

The misconception that debating is an archaic skill reserved only for the fee-paying elite or prospective politicians is a safe and predictable one in which to retreat. It is all too easy to dismiss enrichment in more traditional skills such as oracy in favour of a more prescriptive, short-term approach to teaching—a rather bland recipe concocted in the exams pressure cooker.

A lesson spent interacting with your students and getting involved in the debate yourself is worth its weight in gold. Embedding a culture of oracy in your school will undoubtedly require an initial investment of time and energy, but it will also be the discipline that will remind you why you trained to become a teacher in the first place. Oracy is a skill that has the potential to change the lives of all young people irrespective of ability, gender, age or religion. Isn't that a sentiment that we need to champion in schools, now more than ever?

Sarah Spikesley, head of english at Hinchingbrooke School, a state school in Cambridgeshire

Social mobility

The independent sector has always had a strong tradition of public speaking and debating, seen as a training ground for professions such as the law, media and politics. That said, there is scant evidence that private schools are explicitly teaching the skills of oracy more than the state sector (with the exception of some superb examples of the teaching of rhetoric and debate). Rather, more socially advantaged pupils arrive at school with the confidence and skills to put their points forward. The stereotype that is often used here is of the middle-class dining table, where adults invite children to join their conversation, ask their opinion and listen to them. Private education provides the opportunities for these skills to be practised. Their skills are often "caught rather than taught". But these skills can and should be taught in the state school system. When people refer to the sense of entitlement that privately educated students exude, this can partly be put down to their sense that they have a right to speak and be listened to. The belief that their voice matters is a wonderful gift to try to give to all of the students coming through our state education system.

Geoff Barton talks about his experience of debating, as headmaster of King Edward VI School, and how it helps the "word poor" to take on the habits of the "word rich", teaching them the language of power, which "tends to prize precision, fluency, formality":

> My interest in debating is to do what we can to recreate that culture of conversation, of controlled verbal dispute, of connecting abstract ideas to our own experience and making it all accessible to youngsters who may not have a dining table in their house, let alone conversations across it with an adult each day.[12]

Formal oracy activities, such as Parliamentary Debates or Mock Trials, encourage a formal register of speech. When a student is called on by a chairperson to propose a motion, they are speaking as themselves, but to an extent they are in role. Teachers can support them with the use of academic vocabulary and with scaffolds that promote formal or even parliamentary discourse. For example, "The honourable member of the opposition has put forward an argument that…, but that argument can be countered with the evidence that…". Hearing this language used by their peers and having the chance to model it themselves take away the sense of intimidation that can accompany formal speech and are empowering for young people.

The Social Mobility and Child Poverty Commission identified soft skills as a barrier to social mobility and particularly highlight spoken communication skills. A report from the commission in 2015 on barriers to entering the elite professions found that "elite firms define 'talent' according to a number of factors such as drive, resilience, strong communication skills and above all confidence and 'polish'".[13] Allowing pupils to develop their fluency, formality and finesse through regular practise of critical oracy will stand them in good stead for their future careers.

Ultimately, it is about making sure that no child's life chances are narrowed because they do not have the language, the confidence or the skills to converse and present in a variety of situations.

Lewis Iwu, director of the Fair Education Alliance and himself a former debater and debate coach, said that for him debating in schools was "about being able to unleash the potential of young people and giving disadvantaged kids the ability to navigate the world".[14]

Readiness for civic participation

The skills and confidence needed to articulate your thoughts, along with the belief that you have the right to have your voice heard, have always been important for civic participation. The prospective MP, town councillor, trades union leader or residents' association rep will need to speak for the people they represent, and many of the best will be able to do so powerfully and persuasively. But even those who do not wish to lead should not feel a barrier to participating. To attend a town council planning meeting and to stand up and express yourself on proposed changes to your local community can be too daunting to many who have been given no training or opportunity to practice and have not been educated in a culture in which their voice matters. To stand on the street and engage passersby with your petition or to knock on doors canvassing for your political party of choice requires you to argue your case and defend it against often hostile challenge. To give all young people these skills is an act of enfranchisement.

Indeed, the 21st century poses civic challenges that have never been seen before, and we must equip the next generation to deal with them. Whether they help us to spot fake news, resist radicalisation or avoid trolling, good argumentation skills are

As a debating novice, I was perplexed by the duality existing in things and unable to comment on it because I lacked not only the confidence, but the skill set to do so, the set of skills being analysis, comparison and critique—even of self. Only by practicing did these skills become intuitive in the way I processed information, and soon I was applying these skills to everyday life. Daily activities became worthy of questioning as well as issues such as patriarchy and Brexit. It is the art of debating that can accommodate our need not only to understand the world we live in, but also to challenge it. We, as young people, must be able to recognise the bifurcation of beliefs in order to either accept them as peacefully coexisting or see them as a problem in dire need of resolution—for the sake of our society. Debating changed my life by allowing me to recognise how I can use my voice, but moreover the power of it. The power of questioning in turn leads only to a more profound understanding of things. Debating is not only a way of thinking but a necessary mode of communication. It is the vaccine for ignorance and promotes interactivity, which I have found to break trends of arrogance and bigotry. It promotes politeness and eloquence of speech, which are, much like other skills acquired from debating, transferable and the basis of any future career, and thus beneficial for everyone irrespective of the occupation they desire. Debating is necessary to navigate through this world as a confident, articulate, open-minded person.

Year 11 student from Clapton Girls' Academy in Hackney

an armour in today's world. Avoiding ad hominem attacks, demanding evidence and considering alternate views are useful approaches with which to start. Critical faculties must be developed to interrogate the material that is put before us, especially on social media. A 2018 survey by the Literacy Trust found that only 2% of children and young people in the UK had the critical literacy skills they need to tell if a news story is real or fake.[15] The next generation, given the right skills, can raise the standards of public discourse.

Importance of constructive disagreement

Creationists v evolutionists, pro-lifers v pro-choicers, radicals v moderates, conservatives v liberals—there will always be people we disagree with, other "tribes". The ability of opposing groups to communicate is crucial to social cohesion. Politics in the UK (and the USA and continental Europe) is diverging more as major parties have fled the centre ground. The Brexit referendum revealed deep divides and was a wake-up call to engage with, and not dismiss, large parts of the country where people felt disenfranchised. Schools can instil a culture in which we respect those we disagree with and are tolerant of diverging views. They can give young people the skills and the expectation to engage in reasoned debate, not to resort to abuse or violence. Equally, schools can encourage them to seek out dialogue with those outside their circle, not to close their ears to opposition. The way we now consume media and organise our society and time can make it possible to never venture outside our echo chamber and to feel increasingly alienated from those "other" to us. Comprehensive schools are naturally diverse places—and perfect places to facilitate exchanges of views. Schools in which the pupil population is less diverse may need to make a special effort to invite speakers in who can challenge deeply held views and add to the plurality of ideas.

There is a current culture in some universities and pockets of society that seeks to ban controversial speakers, set up "safe spaces" where ideas cannot be voiced and attempt to block any opposition to the dominant culturally acceptable views. This seems to come mainly from noble desires to protect marginalised groups from offence and to refuse to legitimise diverging views by allowing them a platform. This may be the right response to the most extreme of views, but it holds dangers when it marginalises large pockets of society and shuts down dialogue. I would like to see the pupils we educate in our schools today relish the opportunity to invite those they disagree with to their university—if not to seek to talk to them, understand them and change their views, then just to challenge them publicly. I would like the next generation to consider that it may be better that someone encounters alternative views in a public debate, where fake evidence can be weeded out and prejudices can be exposed, rather than online with nothing to challenge their persuasive rhetoric and fake facts. And I would like liberals to see the danger of putting protecting people from offence above freedom of speech. Any political group can use this defence, once it is a social norm, and who gets to decide who is banned? Constructive disagreement is such a crucial part of our democracy in the way laws are passed in Parliament, the way court cases are decided and the way our politicians are held to account by the media. Let's protect that freedom of speech and the desire to debate with our opponents, starting in the classroom.

> I believe that healthy debate within the classroom is vital to a student's learning. I maintain that the greatest way to teach is to encourage debate. This is because it forces the students, who would otherwise simply be listening and reading (passively absorbing knowledge), to think around a subject; to truly understand a topic you need to argue its case. This is the same reason that for any debate I am involved in, given the choice, I will always argue the side I oppose in reality; this is because debate allows those involved to truly understand other points of view, rather than seeing them through our own biased beliefs. If you want a class of students who understand the topic, rather than simply being able to regurgitate the topic, then classroom debate is a must.
>
> **Iain Lynn, Year 12 student and graduate of the first Up for Debate programme in 2016**

Character education

There is a growing emphasis on character education in our schools. Definitions vary, and the exact list of "mindsets" or "learning dispositions" differs across institutions, but most concentrate on the same areas, regardless of the names used. PiXL Edge, the character education programme of the PiXL Club, uses LORIC (Leadership, Organisation, Resilience, Initiative and Communication). Communication skills are, of course, the most obvious match, but in fact all of these skills can be developed by regularly taking part in debates. In the national oracy programme Up for Debate, which The Noisy Classroom has developed with PiXL Edge, all five are emphasised: critical oracy helps develop the leadership skills to inspire, motivate and listen carefully to others; pupils must organise their time and material to prepare for the task; resilience is built by the practice of being assertively challenged and learning to defend, or amend, one's views without taking the

We initiated debate in the borough through the gifted and talented programme. It was a crowded curriculum, and it seemed to be working on soft skills that didn't initially equate to clear exam outcomes, but as debate became more embedded in schools, the benefits became more obvious. Students started to view speaking in a different way. They might comment on the way something was said as much as they might talk about the content. In schools where teachers were more proactive with debate, students were queuing up for lunchtime debates; speaking became a spectator sport. In class, students were able to drop into a debate format at short notice, and parts of lessons could be explored in ways they could not before.

All of the teachers involved with the programme were amazed how resilient students were. Instead of being overwhelmed, they quickly understood the rules of the game, and that's exactly what it became. I remember going to see a history lesson that slipped into some informal debate. I could see what the teacher was doing in terms of direction and learning outcomes, and because the rules of debate were used, students listened and interacted in a really polite, measured way. At the end, one student was particularly smug that they had "managed to get away without doing any work all lesson". I quizzed him about the main points of the lesson, which he dutifully fed back. It was only then he realised he had spent the whole lesson learning.

If you have concerns about how useful or effective debate and increased oracy are in the classroom, put your concerns to one side, and give it a try. I am confident the response from your students will confirm you have made the right choice. The benefits in behaviour, classroom management, opportunities for assessment for learning, orally upscaling differentiation and just the visible lift you will see in your students' confidence and willingness to contribute will make it a worthwhile endeavour.

Jon Evans, former Gifted and Talented lead at the Hackney Learning Trust

challenges personally; students must show initiative in these pupil-led activities; and, of course, communication skills are built through instruction in and practice of talk-based tasks.[16]

Mental health and well-being

There have been many links made among mental health, well-being and oracy. One study found that 64% of 7–14 year olds referred to psychiatric services had SLCN and 40% of these were previously unidentified.[17] In addition, 60% of young offenders and two-thirds of pupils at risk of exclusion from school have been found to have SLCN.[18] While it is unrealistic to claim that the odd debate in your classroom can mitigate against these facts, a culture of oracy in schools can help students to express themselves verbally, listen empathetically to others, and have the words and the confidence to ask for help. It can provide more opportunities for students with SLCN to be identified and supported. It can give young people the skills they need to fully participate in their wider community and remove barriers to pursuing their interests and passions. It can help them to communicate positively with friends and family.

Student engagement

Debating, Mock Trials, Hot Seating, and the other activities in this book are fun! Students are active and engaged; they are stretched and challenged; they can feel as if they are taking part in games, and yet they are still learning—improving their knowledge, understanding and skills. Noisy classrooms are vibrant, lively, high-energy places, and they can encourage students to engage with the subject matter and to delve deeper than they otherwise would. Studies have shown that pupils report higher levels of engagement when involved in classroom debating, and my personal experience certainly backs this up as long as the activities are structured. Often rule-bound, oracy-based activities are popular and provide an important change of pace from silent reading and writing. These structured activities can also be great levellers. In free-flowing group discussions or class discussions based on a hands-up approach, a minority of pupils will dominate. In a debate, everyone will have their three minutes to speak, and nobody will have longer. Other activities give all pupils specific roles that ensure everyone contributes.

Benefits for the teacher

From a pragmatic perspective, the use of increased critical oracy can contribute to a reduced teacher workload, as marking is done on the spot, rather than in a stack of books later that night. Running a set-piece oracy unit (such as on formal debating) with key stage 3 classes at a time when your examination classes generate a lot

I've been debating for just over a year now, and it has become a big part of my personality and one of my main interests and passions. Although a year may be a short time, I feel as an individual I have learnt a lot from debating. My confidence has developed hugely. Things such as talking in assemblies no longer seem anywhere near as intimidating. When I do have to deliver speeches or even read text in front of class, I'm always thinking about my tone and eye contact and how I can develop my style and structure. Working with two other debaters has also developed my teamwork skills because we all rely on each other when debating against other people. Not only has debating given me several skills, but also it has empowered me to share my opinion on topical things. Due to debating, I am more in touch with current affairs—for example, how the prison system works and Brexit. Having had debates about these in a previous Up For Debate competition, I now find myself bringing up points from the debate in conversation, and I am now generally more intrigued when the topic comes up in the news. I'm grateful for the opportunity to become part of the debating community, and I cannot imagine my life without it.

Year Ten student from Redden Court School in Romford

of marking and planning can be an excellent way to better husband teacher time whilst ensuring that all classes are still engaged in rigorous academic pursuit.

But pragmatics aside, the best argument to put to teachers would be the excitement of a noisy classroom. Working with engaged and enthusiastic students who are expressing themselves and arguing about the fundamentals of your subject is an energising and joyful experience. One lesson of active, passionate debate on Shakespeare would be enough to sustain me through many lessons of past exam paper practice.

Notes

1 Argument-Centered Education, *Research basis*. Available at: http://argumentcenterededucation.com/impact/research-basis/ (Accessed: September 2018).

2 Akerman, R., and Neale, I. (2011) *Debating the Evidence: An International Review of Current Situation and Perceptions*, Reading, UK: CFBT Education Trust.

3 Education Endowment Foundation (2018) *Collaborative learning*. Available at: https://educationendowmentfoundation.org.uk/evidence-summaries/teaching-learning-toolkit/collaborative-learning/.

4 Quigley, A. (2018) *Closing the Vocabulary Gap*, Abingdon, UK: Routledge.

5 British Chamber of Commerce (2014) *Annual Workforce Survey*.

6 CBI (2016) *The Right Combination: CBI/Pearson Education and Skills Survey 2016*, London: CBI.

7 http://www.p21.org

8 Harrell, M., and Barbato, L. (2018) *Great managers still matter: The evolution of Google's Project Oxygen*. Available at: https://rework.withgoogle.com/blog/the-evolution-of-project-oxygen/.

9 Cambridge University, *Transkills: Supporting transition to university.* Available at: https://www.transkills.admin.cam.ac.uk/skills-portal/key-skills-undergraduates (Accessed: August 2018).

10 Weale, S. (2018) "University drop-out rates in UK rise for third successive year", *The Guardian*, 8th March.

11 "Deborah Meier in New York found that a curriculum that places debate and discussion at the core can improve college matriculation and retention by as much as 80% among Title I and at-risk students." Cited by Argument-Centered Education Available at: http://argumentcenterededucation.com/impact/research-basis/.

12 Barton, G. (2016) "Secondary school debating", in *Speaking Frankly*, London: English-Speaking Union and Voice 21, p. 53.

13 Ashley, L., Duberley, J. Sommerlad, H., and Scholarios, D. (2015) *A Qualitative Evaluation of Non-educational Barriers to the Elite Professions*, London: Social Mobility and Child Poverty Commission, p. 6.

14 Iwu, L. (May 2017)"Foreword Motion", *Dialogue*, p.24.

15 National Literacy Trust (2018) *Fake News and Critical Literacy: The Final Report of the Commission on Fake News and the Teaching of Critical Literacy in Schools*, London: National Literacy Trust.

16 See https://www.upfordebate.co.uk.

17 Cohen, N.J. et al. (1998) Language, Achievement, and Cognitive Processing in Psychiatrically Disturbed Children with Previously Identified and Unsuspected Language Impairments. Journal of Child Psychology and Psychiatry. Vol. 39, No 6, pp865–877. Cited in the Bercow 10 Years On report

18 Communication Trust "Communication difficulties—Facts and stats". Available at: https://www.thecommunicationtrust.org.uk/media/2612/communication_difficulties_-_facts_and_stats.pdf.

3 Overcoming barriers to using critical oracy in the classroom

"Writing is more important that speaking and listening."

It is true that the English education system is set up to prioritise writing. With the exception of the odd practical examination and the oral component of foreign languages, the vast majority of the qualifications that students will end up with (at 16 at least) will be graded with reference almost exclusively to a candidate's ability as a writer. The noisy classroom should not be noisy all the time. Of course, teachers need to provide plenty of opportunities for sustained writing, and most of these should include silence or minimal background noise. But there is space for noise too, both for the sake of its own intrinsic value and for the knock-on benefits to writing[1] that occur through the development of thought, understanding and vocabulary. The key is that students do not just "chat" but use the same formal vocabulary and structures in speech that they will be expected to use in their writing. If teachers are loathe to jump straight into oracy-based lessons, then there are plenty of short activities in this book that can be used as starters and plenaries to bookend a writing-focussed lesson.

"Isn't it very hard to control behaviour in an active, noisy classroom?"

Different teachers have different strengths and weaknesses, and all classes have their own challenges too, so there is no one answer to the question. Some teachers find it almost impossible to maintain silence in a classroom and to keep students on focus in written work. In these cases, they may actually find it easier to enthuse and engage classes in more active learning. The noise levels will be higher but so will the number of pupils who are on-task. For teachers who rule their rooms with an iron rod, there is an amount of control that needs to be ceded when developing an oracy-based activity, but that does not mean relinquishing the reins. Clear expectations, detailed instructions, close monitoring, set time limits and agreed methods for bringing the class back to silence all ensure that the teacher is in charge of the dynamics of the room. In fact, many of the activities in this book are so structured that classroom management is not a problem. Amorphous, open-ended tasks such as "Get into groups and discuss X" are largely to blame for the bad reputation that talk has. High-quality, structured oracy activities are significantly easier to control.

"If other staff hear high noise levels, won't they think I'm out of control?"

Some teachers are very self-conscious about the amount of noise coming out of their classroom. They are concerned that to others, a noisy classroom will signal that they are out of control. This is not an unjustified concern—I have had senior managers poke their heads around the door "just to check that everything is ok in here, Miss Newman" when a class has notched up the decibels during Rebuttal Tennis or Table Debates. Many staff are proud of their silent classrooms, and the ability to teach with the door open can be seen as an outward sign of their skill in classroom control. A noisy classroom is not necessarily out of control. Many teachers see staying in control of a noisy classroom as more of a badge of honour than the ability to silence a class. So part of this is about shifting attitudes. But there are other measures that you can do to help. Warn your neighbours that you are going to be running a noisy class so that they know you are in control. Or put a "Noisy Learning in Progress" sign up on your door. Or if you know that it is going to be an especially noisy lesson, then try to book out a drama studio or other space away from the main teaching corridors or even take the lesson outside. Not all of the activities in this book are especially loud. Many of them require only one student speaking at a time while the class listens actively. Where activities do have most of the class speaking together, then you could use a noise meter (handmade or digital) to let the students know if you need them to use lower their voices.

"How can I show evidence of pupil learning if it isn't written in their books?"

This is the sticking point in many schools. Multiple teachers have reported that they cannot dedicate the time they would like to oracy activities because "If it isn't in their books, then it doesn't count". If this is your school culture, you may find your hands tied, but there are still ways to incorporate more oracy into your teaching, even if you cannot do as much as you would wish. If the main body of the lesson is off limits for you, then try these parts: (a) starters and plenaries are good places to introduce short oracy activities; (b) extension activities provide opportunities where critical oracy can challenge the more able; (c) an activity like Hat Debates can be a good one to have up your sleeve when a lesson finishes early; and (d) revision lessons can be an opportunity for set pieces like debates where everyone takes notes in their books.

There are also ways to make sure that an oracy-based activity does leave a trail:

1. Marking: Make sure your assessment of an oracy activity such as a debate or a presentation is as rigorous as that of an essay, and record the marks in your mark book and on slips that pupils can stick into their books

2. Video or audio recording: If you need more of a trail, then set up a camera or a recorder to capture the learning. This also has the advantage that you can play it back to the class or individuals to help them assess their own strengths and weaknesses and you can use the recordings to standardise marking across the cohort.

3. Written evidence in books: Students can prepare the notes for their speeches in their books, stick in key points from their research or include peer- or self-assessment sheets. If a student is taking part more as an active listener, then they can make notes on the key points they have learnt. An oracy-based activity can, with a little extra effort, fill pages in books.

"Shouldn't it just be co-curricular?"

There is a wonderful world of co-curricular oracy activities. There are competitions in public speaking, debating, Model United Nations, Mock Trial and more.[2] Away from competition, schools run thriving debating clubs and give opportunities through school councils and local advocacy. All of this is to be encouraged, but it should not be seen as a replacement for a culture of oracy in the classroom. Building the skills of oracy is necessary for all students, not merely those who self-select. The model is similar to sport: every student takes part in PE whether they like it or not and whether they show any talent or not because there is a benefit to all. Some students show ability and/or passion for sport and are able to pursue this through school teams and clubs. Likewise all students should get the benefits of developing oracy skills, and those who flourish need the opportunity to take this further through co-curricular opportunities. Every school has students on its roll right now who could find that pursuing one of these oracy activities to the top level is life-changing, so the ideal is to take both a curricular and a co-curricular approach.

"Aren't some of these activities too combative?"

I diverge (ironically) from some other proponents of oracy in the classroom in that I am not much of a fan of consensus: in problem-solving, perhaps; in academic study, no. Why should there be a consensus in the group you have constructed on the interpretation of *Richard III* or the main reason for the rise of Hitler or whether the UK should use nuclear energy? There is no consensus in the world of academia as a whole, so why force one on younger pupils? Rather, teach them that challenge is at the heart of academic study and that it is nothing to fear. Others will challenge your ideas, and that is OK. Those others may be your friends, before and after the challenge, and that is OK. *You* are not being attacked—rather, it is merely your intellectual position. Relish the challenge. Keep an open mind—prepare to be persuaded if the challenge convinces you or to defend your position if it does not. Consensus may be found or it may not, and that does not matter.

The argument-centred education movement in the USA cites the Common Core State Standards Research Appendix: argument is "the soul of an education" because when students are engaged in argument about an issue of importance, "something far beyond surface knowledge is required: students must think critically and deeply, assess the validity of their own thinking, and anticipate counterclaims".[3]

Having said that, consensus building is a useful skill in life, especially to working in teams. Opportunities for it to be developed are important, but it does not need to play a role in the majority of pair, group or whole-class discussions. One good place for a consensus-building exercise can be after a debate has finished. Can the class work to find compromise and consensus between the two sides?

"What about particularly quiet or introverted students?"

Some students need no encouragement to talk, whilst others will do anything to avoid it. How do we deal with quiet and/or introverted students in the noisy classroom? The first thing to say is that all students should be required to take part in oracy-based activities even if they hate it. The analogy here is with PE. We do not excuse those who dread PE from taking part because we see the benefits of exercise and hope to impart skill and habits that even the reluctant will take with them to adulthood. Oracy is the same. Not all students will pursue talk-based careers, but they will need to go through interviews, communicate with strangers and articulate their thoughts. Some adults find that they cannot progress through their careers because their communication skills hold them back from taking management positions. Therefore, oracy skills are essential for everyone, not just for the enthusiastic. That said, there is no reason why oracy activities need to intimidate or discomfort a quieter student; there are ways of making a noisy classroom a more hospitable place for the introverted.

1. General group or whole-class discussions where the less loquacious student is required to find an opportunity to put forward their views can be particularly painful. Structured activities where everyone has a role and a turn can be easier.

2. Time to think is crucial. Pupils who are more introverted develop their thoughts before they feel comfortable articulating them, so tactics such as Think-Pair-Share are especially helpful before they have to talk to the class. In *Quiet Power*, Susan Cain endorses this method and also goes further, giving an example of a teacher who asked students first to write out their ideas, second to read each other's ideas and only then to start the discussion.[4]

3. Not everyone finds the same communication situations difficult. Some students who hate group discussion may be very confident in delivering a prepared presentation to the class, so try to provide a range of different activities.

4. Support for talk such as sentence stems (see Appendix C) can allow all students to feel more confident when contributing, as they can follow a set formula.

5. More-extroverted students can be taught to, and rewarded for, bringing quieter peers into the conversation. Many more-introverted students will happily answer a question directed at them but will stay silent unless invited to speak.

"Aren't activities like debating only for the most able pupils?"

When teachers use debates and related activities in the classroom, they often reserve them for the top sets. When the Department for Education commissioned the ESU to set up the London Debate Challenge in 2002, it was placed firmly within the gifted and talented programme. There is no doubt that debating is a superb activity to stretch your most able pupils, and many of the activities in this book are useful extension exercises. Debating is not, however, the reserve of the gifted. Many students who struggle with writing will find that rehearsing their ideas verbally will allow them to develop their thinking and understanding and give them an effective grounding for written work. Debating can help to develop structured thought; technical, formal vocabulary; and deeper analysis. It allows pupils to see good practice from their peers and receive guidance from teachers more immediately than with the essay-writing process. Using scaffolding and sentence stems supports students as they develop their skills. If your pupils are not yet ready to deliver a three-minute speech, then they can build their confidence with short activities such as Boxing Match Debates, Rebuttal Tennis and Hat Debates. Other activities in this book, such as Mock Trials and Argument Stations, have multiple roles, making differentiation easy, but do keep your expectations of all pupils high.

"What about those with specific SLCN?"

There is some extremely high-quality support for those with SLCN in this country, but it is patchy, and it needs more funding and a higher profile to more widely and deeply embed the good practice that it out there. The report

Bercow: 10 Years On summarises the state of SLCN support in the UK.[5] This book does not attempt to specifically address SLCN, but having a culture of oracy in the classroom could contribute by (a) offering additional ways for SLCN to be recognised and referred for support, (b) providing opportunities for the practice of oracy skills and (c) allowing for very structured oracy activities, which are easier to engage in than generalised classroom discussion. For more information about supporting students with SLCN, see https://www.thecommunicationtrust.org.uk/.

"Oracy isn't relevant to my subject"

Teachers of maths and science, of art and music and of PE (amongst others) may feel that oracy is only for English, drama and the humanities. While it is likely that there will be more-extended oracy activities in history than in PE, there is both opportunity and benefit for finding some room for oracy across all subjects. Every subject involves some problem-solving and/or working in a team, and these skills are built effectively through improved oracy. When there are multiple possible approaches to a problem, an experiment, a strategy or a technique, pupils need the ability to discuss these. Additionally, pupils can think about every subject on a meta level and also in terms of how it interacts with society; these discussions can improve pupil engagement. Is modern art really art? Are sports stars paid too much? What are the ethical implications of genetic science? Should music be taught as a subject in schools? Why does maths matter? Teachers report that using critical oracy in this latter way has allowed them to see different sides of their pupils that they never normally see and has given them a chance to communicate their passion for their subject. And, finally, just as we see literacy as being so important that all staff have a duty to develop it—not only for their own subject's examination success but also for the life chances of the pupils—so we believe that oracy should have parity with this.

"Debating and public speaking are elitist activities for posh people"

I wonder what today's teenagers would think of this! If you asked them to name some powerful speakers, they would respond with names like Martin Luther King Jr, Barack Obama and Gandhi for sure. Perhaps they might mention Oprah Winfrey's Oscar acceptance speech or 15-year-old Greta Thurnberg's TED talk on climate change. How many times in their lifetimes have they seen a really powerful speech from a rich, white man? It would not occur to young people that learning to be a persuasive, confident speaker or being able to clearly articulate an argument meant class mimicry—unless you tell them it is! And an older generation will remember the stirring oratory from trade unionist leaders of the past. Public school boys have no monopoly on the skills and confidence necessary to be an effective debater, and it is insidious to suggest otherwise.

"Debating teaches people to be dishonest"

It has become a lazy shorthand to criticise politicians by saying they were in their school's debating society. The inference is they are snake oil salesmen, shorn of all principle, who have learnt the craft of persuasion and who use wily words to manipulate an unsuspecting audience and pursue their own personal ambition. The truth is that the behaviour often being demonstrated by these politicians— not listening to their opponents, failing to answer the questions posed to them and asserting arguments without providing evidence or thorough analysis—would get them knocked out of the first round of any debating competition. Points in debating come from building logical, well-evidenced arguments and comprehensively dealing with the arguments of others. The most successful competitive debaters-turned-politicians are probably John Smith, Donald Dewar and Charles Kennedy—politicians of genuine substance and conviction and not, perhaps, the ones whom many people would suspect.

Far from equipping tomorrow's demagogues, giving all students the skills of debating will help to build a more politically literate society whose members are better able to tell a good argument from a bad one. Giving children the ability to argue both sides of a case does not rob them of their principles; rather, it helps them to see that there is usually more than one side to every story. It saves our young people from the echo chamber of social media. Some people will use their

Six years ago, I started my first British parliamentary-style debate club and have been running the club, organising local competitions and entering national events ever since.

During science lessons, I have attempted to integrate oracy challenge where appropriate. I was initially concerned that by encouraging oracy, I would lose curriculum time and potentially fall behind in terms of content delivery. Also, I believed that my students may feel uncomfortable talking in front of their peers and that this may result in students losing their engagement and passion for science.

Both fears were proven unfounded. Students who did not enjoy writing suddenly found they had a stage to excel. Many male students and students with special education needs and disabilities (SEND) who were disengaged felt they now had a voice (literally!). Science can be an emotive subject, and my students have really benefitted from current scientific issues being debated in the classroom. Their understanding is challenged and then enhanced/stretched.

I would recommend formal and informal debate to other science teachers who are looking to enrich their own schemes of work and challenge the most able. They could even find that students who were previously disengaged rise to the top of the class (and try hard to stay there during other non-oracy-based tasks).

Iain Howes, head of science at Welland Park School, an Ofsted "outstanding" secondary school in Market Harborough, Leicestershire

ability to speak well for ill, but they will do the same with their ability to write convincing prose—and I have never heard anyone say we should not teach writing for this reason.

Notes

1 Kuhn, D., Zillmer, N., Crowell, A., and Zavala, J. (2013) "Developing norms of argumentation: Metacognitive, epistemological, and social dimensions of developing argumentive competence", *Cognition and Instruction*, 31:4, pp. 456–496. In this study, Professor Kuhn and her colleagues showed that high school students enrolled in a Columbia University debate-based curriculum for two years outperformed a control group by 41% on a standardised college-level writing assessment.

2 See https://www.noisyclassroom.com/calendar for opportunities.

3 Argument-Centered Education, *Argument and the common core.* Available at: http://argumentcenterededucation.com/argument/argument-and-the-common-core/ (Accessed: September 2018).

4 Cain, S. (2016) *Quiet Power: Growing Up as an Introvert in a World That Can't Stop Talking*, New York: Penguin.

5 ICAN (2018) *Bercow: 10 years On.* Available at: https://www.bercow10yearson.com.

The role of senior leaders and teachers in a school of noisy classrooms

The role of senior leaders

Cross-curricular literacy is a well-established concept, and oracy deserves the same profile at a whole-school level. Yet 57% of teachers say they have not received any training in oracy in the last three years.[1] Here are some suggestions to raise the profile of oracy in your school:

- Appoint an oracy lead staff member.
  The majority of schools have a literacy lead. An oracy lead can be just as effective for co-ordinating a cross-school approach to oracy, monitoring its success and keeping its profile high.

- Provide continuing professional development in oracy for all staff.
  Allowing successful practitioners to share their best practice, inviting in outside experts or sending targeted members of staff to external events can revitalise oracy practise in your school and ensure that all staff feel confident and skilled in delivering a range of activities.

- Produce school-wide guidelines and expectations for effective oracy.
  Students will thrive if they are given consistent guidelines across the curriculum. Although there are some subject-specific variants, schools can agree on core expectations on, for example, use of formal vocabulary, answering in whole sentences, displaying listening behaviours and effective group work.

- Conduct an oracy audit.
  A reflective school will want to know where it is starting from before it embarks on a journey to improve oracy standards. What activities are happening now? Can they be mapped by subject, year group and time of year? Which subjects or

individual teachers are leading the way? What skills are your students strong in and where do they need to develop?

- Introduce an oracy grade or judgement on pupil reports.
  Reporting on oracy will focus the minds of teachers, pupils and parents and raise the profile of oracy across the school community.

- Run a school-wide No Pens Day.
  The Communication Trust run an annual national No Pens Day but a school can call their own whenever suits them. On the day, all teachers must run all of their lessons without any written exercises. This can be an engaging day which focuses people's minds on different teaching methods which they can use throughout the year.

- Widen co-curricular opportunities.
  There are many choices for co-curricular activities with an oracy focus. Schools can run debating clubs, public speaking clubs or philosophy or politics societies which are run through discussion. Schools could run their own inter-form or inter-house competitions in debating and public speaking and/or enter some of the national programmes run in debate, public speaking, mock trials, Model United Nations and Model Parliament. Schools can also offer opportunities for advocacy through school councils.

- Give time to oracy during tutor time, on off-timetable days and in sixth form skills or enrichment programmes.
  Many schools fit opportunities in to explicitly teach and develop oracy skills in these out-of-lesson learning opportunities.

- Form an assessment policy that recognises marks gained from debates, presentations and other oracy activities.
  Teachers are expected to fill mark books and will feel more empowered to run oracy-based lessons if they are supported with an assessment policy which recognises these activities.

- Consider how you structure assemblies, tutor time, parent-teacher meetings, school governance etc. to allow opportunities for student voice.
  Students do not have to be passive in these school events. Some schools look to maximise the opportunities that their students have to speak. For example could a class or an individual student run an assembly or could it be led with pair or group work involved?

- Consider accredited assessments (such as those offered by the English Speaking Board) as part of your curriculum and qualification offer.
  Students can be given formal recognition of their communication skills if they take part in accredited assessment. This can lead to better teaching of oracy skills and students taking their own development more seriously Additionally,

a qualification is a useful way of evidencing skill in later job applications. The English Speaking Board offers qualifications in speech, debating and interview skills, amongst others.

- Provide opportunities for staff to improve their own oracy skills in areas such as questioning and exposition.

  Continuing Professional Development can look at the teachers' own oracy skills and seek to improve upon it, as well as looking at their capacity to run oracy-based lessons for pupils. This is an area where coaching can be especially effective.

- Regularly invite outside speakers to your school so that pupils have a chance to hear and question people with different backgrounds, professions, viewpoints and expertise.

  Many charities, NGOs, religions, businesses and community groups will provide speakers to visit your schools. Take up as many of these opportunities as you can to ignite debate within your school. Parents can also be a useful resource here, as can allowing teachers the chance to speak outside of lessons on their areas of interest.

The implementation of a whole-school oracy initiative seemed, when we began it, to be a formidable proposition. While colleagues who taught English and humanities-related subjects were easily won over, the same could not be said of those whose academic interests seemed distant from traditional skill sets associated with formal debate. This skepticism, underpinned by a much-cited imperative to "get through the syllabus", meant that we faced initial difficulties. Persistence paid off, as did the provision of low-stakes, high-impact whole-school CPD. Elevating the profile of pupil talk across the full spectrum of school activities served to render it less unfamiliar, while reconfiguring the focus of cross-faculty pedagogic discussion helped also to promote uptake by our staff—for a year, we made speaking skills the centrepiece of our strategy for teaching and learning. Slowly, the school's culture changed, and, as it did so, the multiple benefits of a curriculum premised upon oracy became increasingly apparent. Several years on, our pupils are more confident and far better equipped for collaborative learning; an unanticipated benefit of our programme has been that the quality of group work across the school has been considerably enhanced even when it does not have an ostensible focus on speaking. Moreover, oracy has helped us to dissolve some of the walls between our subjects. Better than ever before, our pupils show a predisposition against the "silo thinking" engendered by a nonspeaking curriculum. Their ability to link ideas and disciplines has been strengthened, and all teachers, irrespective of their subject, are quick to welcome it.

Chris Wolsey, deputy head at Ibstock Place School, an independent co-educational school in south-west London

The role of teachers

The teacher as model

Do not forget your role as a model of good oracy habits. For some students, you will provide their main opportunity to see effective oracy in practice from an adult. Evaluate your own strengths and weaknesses, and make a conscious effort to display high-quality, academic talk in exposition and questioning. Alex Quigley points to how important it is to use "slightly bookish" language[2] and to use the vocabulary and structures that students will need in your particular discipline. Geoff Barton writes that "Great teachers don't just teacher their subject: they use and demonstrate the language of the expert".[3]

The teacher as controller of the noise levels

Make sure that you can immediately silence a noisy classroom when you want to, ideally without having to shout over the noise! An agreed system in which, for example, the teacher raises their hand to signal that the students should return to silence usually works. Some teachers use a noise meter on a screen that lets the class know whether an activity should be silent, involve minimal talking or be full-on noisy.

The teacher as task setter

The instructions you give will determine the focus of the task. How long do students have? Do they have specific roles? Are there outcomes? Have you provided a list of questions to discuss? Sentence starters or vocabulary that they must use? An extension task if they feel they have finished? The activities in this book are very focussed, but the setup you provide to ensure that the class knows the exact expectations is key.

The teacher as monitor

An oracy-focussed activity is not a chance to sit at your desk and catch up on marking! When the class is working in pairs or groups, be sure to be on your feet circulating, monitoring and intervening when necessary. Challenging pupils, ensuring that everyone is on task and nudging the direction of a conversation can all make a difference in ensuring that the talk in your classroom is of high quality.

The teacher as assessor

Not all oracy-based activities need be marked, but many should be. Individual or group presentations, debates and Hot Seating, for example, are excellent activities for which you can record pupils' attainment. If an activity is to be marked, you must decide and communicate in advance how many of the marks will be for content and how many for other oracy skills. (See Appendix F for an example of a marking scheme for debates.) You should verbally offer formative and summative assessment throughout the lesson.

The teacher as instructor/coach

You must make sure that pupils have the skills they need to engage with the set task. Do they need to see the activity modelled by you or already competent students? Do they need scaffolding or help with sentence stems? Once the activity has started, do they need coaching to help them improve? You should be ready to support pupils in moving towards best practice: "Say it again; say it better." "Try expressing that idea in a full sentence." "Can you build on that idea in more depth?" "Can you use academic language to describe that?"

The teacher as evaluator

Whether you are teaching or conducting lesson observations, you should have a set of criteria by which to judge if the activity has been a success. Here are some ideas of what could be included in those criteria:

1. Are all the pupils in your class speaking up? Are there any particular groups (e.g. EAL, SEND) who are not getting involved?

2. Are the pupils responding to what their classmates say, rather than having to have everything mediated through you? In other words, is the talk becoming self-perpetuating?

3. Are pupil contributions to the discussion properly developed? Do they go beyond just a couple of words or a sentence? Are the pupils using the appropriate register? Do they use the specialist vocabulary associated with their subject/topic?

4. Are the spoken contributions of high quality? On topic? Insightful? Well informed?

5. Do the pupils seem engaged in their learning?

6. Is the quality of talk improving over time?

Ways to judge these criteria include the following:

1. Teacher observation of the activity.

2. Pupil reaction. Ask them, "Are you enjoying this? Does it help you to learn? Why?"

3. Assessment of the written work that derives from the lessons in which talk has been prominent. Has the quality of the written work improved?

Debate was something that I saw only as an extracurricular activity and beyond what I had the capacity to do as a teacher. However, upon entering a debate competition in 2016 with some key stage 3 students, I was able to see that debate was not as intimidating as I first thought. Also, I realised that it could be a powerful tool inside the classroom. There is a vast array of informal and formal debate methods available (many of which are detailed in this book), and I used them to introduce debate within my teaching at all key stages. The engagement of students was and is excellent. Using formats such as Boxing Match, Rebuttal Tennis and Hot Seating allowed the students to explore topics and concepts at a consistently high level and created enthusiasm for students whose strengths did not necessarily sit with writing. Utilising a formal debate structure then became a regular occurrence in my classroom, even with 30 students where all students have a role to play, not just the 3 speakers on each side. I think debate in the classroom allows students the opportunity to have a voice and comment on what we as a society are teaching them. It's also a lot of fun!

Charles Barnett, assistant head and teacher of history at Wensleydale School and Sixth Form in North Yorkshire

The teacher as builder of oracy skills

Should the teaching of oracy be explicit or implicit? Both—the same recipe as for writing!

You should give students regular opportunities to take part in structured oracy activities *and* explicitly teach them the oracy skills needed to ensure that they thrive in these activities. The balance of what you do will depend on your role and subject. Oracy across the curriculum can be seen in the same way as literacy across the curriculum. The English Department is likely to take on most of the burden of teaching explicit skills, and these skills will be supported across all other subjects. A teacher of science will rightly not be expecting to take a lesson out of their time to teach about articulating clearly and using eye contact. Their job can be seen as (a) providing opportunities for students to engage in high-quality talk, (b) emphasising and supporting school-wide oracy standards and (c) providing explicit guidance for subject-specific vocabulary, grammar and tone.

Following are the steps for building oracy skills:

1. Set expectations: Have guidelines that are shared and displayed on what makes high-quality talk.

2. Monitor: Make sure that you are circulating and listening to group/pair interactions. Consider using students to help you with this.

3. Encourage reflection: Give students explicit feedback on their oracy skills, and encourage them to reflect on their strengths and weaknesses.

4. Provide practice: If you teach one unit in which oracy skills are used and then move on to the next thing, do not expect these skills to stick. The key thing is for the students to become immersed in a culture of high-quality talk where they build their skills with support and reflection.

The activities in this book are designed to give you a toolkit of talk—to facilitate an oracy culture in your classroom and to allow you to teach the curriculum through effective, high-quality talk. Chapter 7 gives some exercises for explicitly developing oracy skills, and there are scaffolds and sentence stem support in the appendices, but this book is not designed as a handbook for explicitly teaching oracy. If you desire more information on this, the Oracy Framework developed by the Faculty of Education at the University of Cambridge and Voice 21—which divides the skills into four strands: physical, linguistic, cognitive and social/emotional—can provide a useful starting point for isolating the different skills that can be explicitly taught and supported.

Notes

1 Millard, W., and Menzies, L. (2016) *Oracy: The State of Speaking in Our Schools.* London: LKMco and Voice 21.
2 Quigley, A. (2018) *Closing the Vocabulary Gap*, Abingdon, UK: Routledge.
3 Barton, G. (2013) *Don't Call It Literacy! What Every Teacher Needs to Know About Speaking, Listening, Reading and Writing*, Abingdon, UK: Routledge.

5 Troubleshooting

Running high-quality talk-based activities in your classroom can feel intimidating if you are not used to it. However, it is not nearly as hard as some teachers might fear. The activities in this book are tried and tested, and you should feel confident to give all of them a go. As with any classroom practice, the more embedded it becomes for both teacher and pupil, the smoother it will run. That said, there are some issues that you may encounter in the early days, depending on the classes with whom you are working. Happily, each of them can be speedily resolved.

"Debates and discussions turn into full-blown arguments."

There is a fine line between passionate, heated debate and a level of conflict that is not welcome in a classroom. Whilst it is unlikely that you will cross this line debating *Hamlet* or the Glorious Revolution, it could be an issue if you are discussing abortion in religious education (RE) or genetic engineering in science. Assigning roles rather than allowing students to pick sides can be helpful here, as it serves to depersonalise the issue. Some students may initially refuse to argue against their beliefs, but they can usually be (reluctantly) persuaded. The expectation must be set before any discussion, and upheld as it progresses, that only arguments can be attacked; no personal insults are permitted. Also, warn the students not to dismiss the other side's arguments as "stupid" or "ridiculous", but, rather, encourage them to deconstruct the arguments that they hear and show *why* they reject the point. Different teachers will tolerate (and indeed welcome) different levels of heated engagement with the debate, so make sure the students know your expectations. Decide whether the audience permitted to say "Hear, hear" and "Shame" or whether its members must stay silent. If the latter, could they be given "Agree" and "Disagree" (or green and red) cards to hold up to express their support and dissent?

"I set a speaking task and the class is quickly quiet."

This is probably the worst thing that can happen in an oracy-based activity! The first thing to check is whether the task you have set is appropriate. Do the students have enough knowledge and/or understanding to engage in the discussion? Was there enough material to discuss so as to keep the activity going? Then think about whether your instructions were full enough. Does the class know what you expect of them? You may need to make your instructions more specific by, for example, replacing "Discuss the pros and cons of appeasement" with "Discuss three pros and three cons of appeasement". The next possibility, especially if the exercise never really gets going, is that the class needs more support to engage in the activity. Do your pupils need prompts, sentence starters or word banks to help them? Do they need to see the activity modelled before they will feel confident to take part? If you are moving from a silent classroom model to a noisy classroom, it may take the pupils some time to build up their stamina for spoken activities. Start with short, focussed exercises, and build from there.

"The same few people are dominating discussions."

Many of the activities in this book are designed to stop this from happening. This problem is worst when teachers are running whole-class discussions with a hands-up approach, rather than calling on pupils to keep everyone involved, or when group work is set with no roles within it. The structured, focussed activities in Part II build in turn-taking and individual roles to prevent confident students from dominating discussion.

If you are finding that this is still a problem or if you are running a less-structured group discussion, then make sure that the class knows that certain behaviours beyond speech-making will be rewarded. These behaviours include asking questions of others, bringing more quiet students into the discussion and listening carefully. Appointing a chair for each group who understands that part of their role is to get everyone speaking can also be helpful, and this may sometimes be an appropriate role for dominant students. These same techniques should be helpful for supporting more-introverted students in contributing to discussions. Also, check that your pupils feel that they are in a safe, positive space where mistakes are encouraged. This environment will encourage everyone to get involved.

"My students have strong opinions, but they struggle to justify them."

The more your students take part in the activities in this book, the less of a problem this will become. Debating and critical oracy help students to justify their positions because they have to defend them against attack. Teachers can provide them with the skills they need by teaching and modelling the construction of arguments supported with analysis and evidence. Keep asking "Why?" Reading academic texts and opinion pieces will also help to build the habits of argumentation.

"My students' oracy is improving, but I am not seeing the knock-on effect on their writing."

Try mapping an oracy activity directly to a written task. For example, get six groups to prepare a different argument each on an essay question, and ask them to present it orally to the class. Then set the essay as a piece of written work, with each point turned into one paragraph.

   If your students are arguing effectively orally but are still simply describing or narrating on paper without deploying all of the analytical and evidential skills that their spoken contributions exhibited, then try to get them to imagine an opponent who is disagreeing with everything they write. It is their job to persuade this unreasonable critic of their points—and they will need reasoning and evidence to do it.

"Discussions are going off-topic."

Do you have students in your class who will take the opportunity of a paired discussion to talk about anything other than the task? If so—and this is a very typical problem—then you need to circulate during the speaking activity so as to ensure everyone is on-task, just as you would do during a written activity. Your presence is the strongest deterrent to distraction. Activities that are more structured are harder to stray from, so Table Debates, for example, may be more suitable for your class than discussion tasks. Make sure your students know why the activity is relevant and what it is leading to, as this can also help to maintain focus.

"My students are great at talking but not so good at listening!"

Many of the activities in this book reward active listening. Aside from all of the debating activities, one might draw attention to Rebuttal Tennis, On That Point, Mock Trials and many others—they all require critical listening to really engage in the task. Try to make sure your feedback focusses on good listening as much as good speaking so that your students know that it is something you value. If your students are struggling, it is worth taking the time to have an explicit discussion about what good listening is and how they can demonstrate it.

"My classroom gets *too* noisy—nobody can focus and I cannot get the attention of the class when I need it."

There is such as a thing as too much noise in a classroom, even during an oracy activity! If the class is working in pairs or groups, then its members must use "indoor voices". You could use a noise meter (physical or digital, real or imaginary) to let the class know how much noise is expected. It can be helpful to have a signal (such as one arm in the air) to let the class know when you want silence so that you do not have to shout over 30 voices. You can use your signal to remind your class to keep the noise down and then restart the activity if necessary.

"My 'noisy classroom' is generating adverse comment from senior colleagues."

If you know that a lesson is going to be especially noisy, it may be worth booking a drama studio or other space away from the main corridors. If you are in your own classroom, a sign on the door saying "Noisy Learning in Progress" will signal to those walking by that you are in control of the noise. You could also invite colleagues to observe your noisy lessons or ask for a slot in a staff meeting to share the thinking behind noisy pedagogy.

"Some students are articulating ideas that I feel ought to have no place in my classroom."

This is a very tricky area, and to a degree, much will depend on the local context. Different schools and different teachers vary in terms of terms of the tolerance that they will extend to speaking activities and to the points of view that can be expressed within them. Some teachers may welcome a debate in tutor time that examines the pros and cons of mass immigration or the rights and wrongs of abortion, whereas for others, even the framing of the debate would be unacceptable. When setting topics, individuals must stay within their own limits and be mindful of the response of the students and of the wider school community. It may be advisable to seek the opinion of a senior colleague before debating an especially controversial issue. It is worth asking "Does the discussion have a productive outcome, or will it just be toxic views aired with no purpose?" If a topic is being set that could be sensitive, it is worth priming pupils before a debate starts about which arguments may be unacceptable to articulate or which may need real care if they are to be deployed. Do not set a controversial topic "cold"; rather, teach around the issue beforehand.

If teachers find themselves confronted by views that they find unacceptable, then they have a professional responsibility to publicly challenge them. For example, if a history teacher set a debate on appeasement and a student articulated a view that the Holocaust never happened, then this will present an obvious opportunity to publicly engage with that view, to counter it and to explain why it is wrong. If, during a debate, a range of unpalatable views is presented, then consider adjustments to the subsequent teaching programme such that they can be tackled more comprehensively. Certainly, at this point, it would be useful to talk to other colleagues like, for example, the personal, social, citizenship and health education

(PSCHE) team, and the school may also wish to consider the pastoral care options for students who have been offended.

Handled correctly, a controversial debate can be more beneficial than avoiding an issue. Children can build the skills, knowledge and resilience to challenge extremist arguments. They *will* encounter extreme views, probably online, and schools can contextualise these within rational, evidenced discussion.

"Debates and discussions are sidetracked by peripheral issues."

During debates, students sometimes fixate on a minor point or detail, focussing on that, rather than on the significant issues that you wish to be discussed. The specific questions that you set can go some way to averting this kind of problem. A pair activity may be directed to "discuss which of these issues affects the most people" or to "rank these arguments in order of importance and justify why". In a debate, the presence of an audience can help focus speakers' minds on key issues. Remind your speakers to ask "If I win this point, will it help to persuade the audience to support my side overall?" Students can also be encouraged to challenge each other's points not just on their truth but also on their significance. As your pupils build their ability to prioritise arguments in their spoken activities, their written work should also improve.

"How do I implement differentiation in oracy lessons?"

Many of the activities in this book provide natural opportunities for differentiation through the variety of roles they offer. Stretch your most able students in a Mock Trial by making them the lawyers or support the children who are developing their oracy skills in a Boxing Match Debate. Sometimes you may wish to group by ability and set varying tasks. For example, if each group is representing different parties in a Public Meeting, then you can allocate these positions by challenge. On other occasions, mixed-ability grouping will be more appropriate, but roles such as chairperson, ambassador and secretary can be carefully selected.

Differentiation can also be achieved through the level of support material students are given. Some debaters may no longer need the scaffolding sheets (Appendix H) after they have become confident, whereas others may thrive by continuing to use the prompts. Would some of your students benefit from sentence starters or a sheet of key vocabulary?

The activities in this book are all suitable for all abilities. Resist falling into the trap of keeping back debates and related activities for the top sets!

Part II

What to do in your classroom: The activities

Notes for different subjects on activities and topics

English: In this subject, the skills inherent in critical oracy are as important as the content, so the teacher has significant leeway when choosing topics. Any debate or critical oracy activity will provide practice in using persuasive language and in forming analytical arguments. In this book, we have suggested text-based topics for literature, but debates could equally invoke themes suggested by literary texts (for example, the death penalty from *Measure for Measure*). Alternatively, topics can be linked to non-fiction and media (for example, two opposing newspaper articles studied for bias can provide a good way into a debate).

The humanities and social sciences: These subjects subsist on the academic debates that rage within them. Teachers within this curriculum area understand that almost every facet of the topics that they teach is debatable and that the skills of evaluating different opinions, advancing a well-developed argument and using evidence are crucial to pupils' academic success.

Foreign languages and EAL: What is important here is the opportunity for speaking and listening and for developing new vocabulary. Virtually any topic is a possibility. As such, languages have not been included under the possible topics that are suggested for each activity.

The arts, sciences, mathematics, physical education (PE), design and technology (DT) and computing: It is unlikely that with any single class, you will run a big set-piece activity like a Parliamentary Debate or a Mock Trial more than once a term—or even once a year. However, the shorter activities that are outlined here can be used on a daily or weekly basis to embed a culture of high-quality talk within your classroom. On those occasions when you choose to hold a bigger, set-piece event, it will be a delight to see a side of some of your pupils that is normally hidden from you.

Vocational subjects: Industries have their own internal issues that are ripe for debate. Activities in which students debate topics ranging from the testing of beauty products on animals to the effects of tourism on developing nations can help them consider practical and ethical elements of their future career.

Form tutors/PSCHE: There are many moral, social, political and cultural issues that lend themselves to debate. Some of the shorter activities included here could become regulars in your classroom. However, try to make room for some longer formats as well so as to allow the pupils the opportunity to develop their ideas in more depth.

If want pre-prepared stimulus material for a debate, https://www.noisyclassroom. com has stimulus sheets on a wide range of topics.

Choosing your topics

Many parts of the curriculum for all subjects and age groups will generate topics for discussion and debate. Some of these formats require there to be (at least) two sides of an argument that can be put across. In these cases, it is not essential that you choose a topic where the positions are completely equally weighted as long as there are plausible points on both sides. Make sure your wording of the topic is clear so that everyone is approaching the same question. Define terms if necessary to avoid misunderstandings. For older pupils, looking to past examination papers for inspiration can be fruitful, but equally this can be a space to broaden understanding and context. Noisy classrooms often take on controversial subjects, but make sure you do not choose a topic if you would not be comfortable hearing both sides articulated.

Which activities are right for me?

Formal debate is perhaps the most academically rigorous of all the critical oracy activities in this book. The need to structure a speech around individual points, all of which are analysed and supported by evidence, most directly mirrors the skills needed in essay writing. The fact that all ideas that put forward are challenged allows the issue to be explored in depth, viewpoints to be clarified and refined and multiple interpretations to be considered. Parliamentary Debates and Table Debates deliver on a large number of skills simultaneously. However, it is recognised that they do take up large chunks of class time and sometimes shorter activities are more appropriate. Rebuttal Tennis, Hat Debates and Boxing Match Debates, for example, can provide opportunities to explore an argument but can be fitted into short-burst activities such as starters. Where the main aim is to see an issue from specific viewpoints, then Public Meetings or Question Times may work best; where the aim is to gain a greater understanding of a character, then Hot Seating or Chat Shows can be most relevant. If you are looking to impose greater structure on your pair and group work, then Chapters 10 and 11 provide ideas for that.

6 **Parliamentary Debate**

If your pupils are familiar with Parliamentary Debate, then they will easily be able to adapt both to the other longer formats and to the shorter activities included here, as they will be accustomed to forming arguments, presenting them persuasively and listening critically to others.

This chapter will look at a debating format that provides for three-on-three speakers with three-minute speeches, an audience debate and summary speeches. This format works very well in a classroom setting, but teachers should feel free to vary the number of speakers, the length of speeches or any other feature that will make it more suitable to the class and time frame available (for example, three-minute speeches will not to be long enough for deep analysis in an A Level class). Just make sure that the number of speakers and the times on both sides stay equal in order to keep proceedings fair.

Preparing for debates

Wise schools ensure that all of their pupils are familiar with the rules that govern debating and with the steps that are used to prepare for a debate. Making debating an integral part of every pupil's entitlement means that a teacher of science, French or PE will know that they can set up this sort of activity without having to go through the process of introducing the format and skills to their pupils first. Inducting all pupils into the protocols of debate is usually a task undertaken by the English Department, but it can equally be done through humanities lessons or even through an off-timetable PSCHE day.

If, in your school, your pupils lack this kind of formative knowledge, then you will need to take the time to familiarise your class with the debating process. Happily, however, this is not too onerous a task. If this is the first time your class is debating, then it is a good idea to show them one of the videos of a debate on https://www.noisyclassroom.com. The clips will quickly give them a sense of the format, rules and expectations of debating. If you think that a two- to three-minute speech is out of reach for your pupils, then start them with Hat Debates and Rebuttal Tennis to build their skills.

Once this knowledge is established, debate is both a planning- and a marking-light activity that one can return to time after time, confident that it is also an activity that provides pupils with an academically rigorous experience. Preparing for a debate is an activity that may be set to a group within a class as either an extension activity or a homework task. Alternatively, a teacher may ask a whole class to prepare simultaneously for a variety of debate topics. If this latter model is chosen then the process might look something like this.

To start, divide the class (let's say 24 students) into eight groups of three. If you do not want every pupil to give a speech, then the groups can be bigger. The extra pupils can be involved in preparation, chairing and timekeeping, and they can give speeches supporting their side in the audience debate. Each of these groups will be asked to prepare either a proposition or an opposition argument for one of four topics. Once the sides have been allotted, they will need to go through the following five stages in their groups

Generate ideas

In this step, the groups should generate as many ideas as they can to support their side. We recommend giving the class some silent time first and then time when the group members can share their ideas with one another. One group member might act as a scribe, or the group can be given a large piece of a paper and a pack of sticky notes on which they can capture their ideas.

Organise these ideas

In this step, the groups evaluate the ideas that they have generated. Are there any that are similar and should be grouped together? Are there any that contradict and cannot both be used? Are there any that are irrelevant or too insignificant to be used? The group must also prioritise the ideas, putting the most important ones at the start of the debate. Each main speaker will require two or three arguments each, so the points will need be divided up. The second speaker should not repeat or contradict the points of first; rather, they must add new points in supporting their side of the debate.

Sometimes the points will divide up thematically. For example, the first speaker will look at the individual and the second at society. Alternatively, the first speaker might consider the political and the second the economic. It is important to note that there should be enough argument in the first speech as to "prove" the proposal. Otherwise it is "hung". For example, in a debate in which the first speaker seeks only to set out a problem, leaving it to the second speaker to present the solution, there is a problem. After all, the first opposition speaker could agree entirely with the problem. The first speaker would "prove" nothing.

Structure the speeches

All debate speeches should use the following structure —or at least something very similar to it:

Introduction (What do we stand for today?)
Preview (my three points will be...)
Rebuttal (or definition for the very first speaker)
Point One
Point Two
Point Three
Reminder (my three points were...)
Conclusion (vote for us!)

Pro forma speech sheets (see Appendix H) can be downloaded to support this structure, or they can be displayed on the whiteboard at the front of the classroom while the groups make notes.

Develop arguments

In this step, the speakers must take the initial idea for the point and turn it into an argument. As they do this, they should follow a straightforward sequence:

Point: the name of their point
Explanation: the analysis explaining this point
Evidence: an example, study or piece of evidence backing up their point

There is a worked example of this speech and argument structure in Appendix D. However, if your school teaches paragraph structure for essay writing in a slightly different way, then you are advised to follow your institution's prescribed approach.

The whole group can be involved in fleshing out the detail of the analysis and helping with examples. The pupils should not write their speeches out word-for-word; rather, they should use short notes. This is a speaking activity, not a writing and reading out loud activity. That said, pupils may want to pen a few rhetorically pleasing phrases to use at the start and end of their speeches, and if this does not come naturally to them, they should plan which structural connectives they will use as they deliver their speech: e.g. "To begin with", "Furthermore" and "Finally" (see Appendix C for more ideas of sentence starters and connectives).

Make final preparations

Whilst the first two speakers are making their notes, the summary speakers and any other members of the group can start to anticipate what the other side is going to say. They should start to plan rebuttals, which they can share with their teammates. If you are allowing access to technology or other resources, then the pupils can also be asked to research good evidence to help the main speakers. The summary speakers will have to be responsive to the other team whilst they are on their feet, but they can make notes of the points on their own side, which they can use to remind the audience of how persuasive their team has been.

If you have a large class of younger pupils and need an activity for some students to undertake while the main speakers are preparing their speeches, one possibility is to have them design posters or placards that can be displayed or waved during the debate. This may serve to focus attention on the different ways in which we seek to persuade or get our points across when we do not have the main stage.

If there is time, the main speakers can rehearse their speeches in their groups. This can build their confidence and help them to check on their timing.

Holding debates

Once all of the preparation is complete, you will be ready to run your debate. It will take 20–25 minutes. The classroom should be set up as in Figure 6.1.

Each debate will need a chairperson to keep order and call on the speakers and a timekeeper to manage the timings of the debate.

When ready, you should introduce the chairperson. All being well, you should not need to intervene again. The chairperson will call on the speakers in the following order:

First Proposition
First Opposition
Second Proposition
Second Opposition
Audience Debate
Opposition Summary Speaker
Proposition Summary Speaker

The summary speakers switch order to allow the proposition to have the final say.

The timekeeper will make the following audible noises with a bell, a gavel or a good hit on the table:

30 seconds: one knock to signal that points of information are allowed
2.30: one knock to signal no more points of information are allowed and to warn the speaker that they have 30 seconds remaining
3.00: a double knock to signal the end of the allotted time
3.15: continual knocking until the speaker sits down

Points of information

Points of information (POIs) are a way of allowing speakers to interject during the opposing team's speeches. They make the debates more interactive and encourage active listening even after individual pupils have given their speech. Some

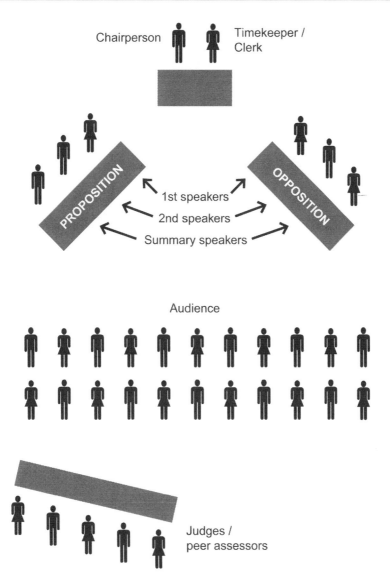

Figure 6.1 Classroom set up for a debate.

teachers do not use them when they are first introducing debates, but if you show a video in which they feature, then your students will probably want to add them straightaway.

Here is how they work. POIs can be offered to speakers on the opposing team. They are a way of putting the speaker on the spot by posing a question or offering a counterargument that needs to be responded to directly. They should be 5-10 seconds long.

To offer a POI, pupils should rise from their chair and say "Point of information" or "On that point". They should then wait. The speaker will say "Accepted" or "Declined". If declined, the pupil offering must sit down and try again later. If accepted, the pupil offering should make their point quickly and then sit down again while the main speaker provides an answer. Those pupils who offer POIs have no right of response to the answer that they receive.

Speakers do not have to accept any POIs, but they will be less persuasive if they choose not to engage. Our advice is simple: in a three-minute speech, a typical speaker should take one or two points. Accepting more than three will diminish the time available for exposition of the speaker's points.

The timekeeper will make an audible signal after 30 seconds and before the last 30 seconds of a speech. The times before the first signal and after the second signal are protected from POIs so that the speaker can introduce and conclude uninterrupted. In most formats, the summary speaker cannot be interrupted by POIs at all, but teachers should adjust this requirement if it suits their need.

At the end of the debate

A vote should be taken. (Indeed, some teachers like to take a vote before the debate as well. The result can serve to stimulate a discussion at the end of the debate about what changed the pupils' minds.)

You should correct any factual errors that were presented during the debate and tease out any missed arguments or material that you would (or would not) want repeated in an essay.

If there is the chance, the debaters will benefit from on-the-spot verbal feedback about their performance—from you and/or their peer assessors. The familiar formula of "two stars and a wish" may be appropriate.

If you have concerns with the adversarial nature of debate, then you might finish with a consensus-building exercise. Can the students find the common ground between the two sides? Can they suggest compromises and find a middle ground?

Engaging the whole class during the debate

One of the barriers teachers report to us in using formal debate in the classroom is that not enough pupils are engaged on-task during the proceedings. This need not be the case. Here are some ideas to satisfy any lesson observer that your whole class is learning.

Peer assessors

Provide all of the audience members with a peer-assessment form, and have them become judges. They can be asked to look at all aspects of the debate. Alternatively, you could divide them up, with some of them examining the way in which language was used, some of them thinking about the content of the speeches and others considering the quality of delivery of each speech.

Journalists

Turn your audience into the press gallery. As either a homework task or a follow-up lesson activity, your pupils can be asked to write a newspaper report of the debate. This will require them to listen closely and take careful notes during the debate. For even more of a challenge, give different students different biases or perspectives from which to write their report.

Essay writers

If the pupils know that, having staged a debate, they will be asked to write an essay on the same topic, then the debate becomes their research. The closer they listen to it and the more carefully they take notes, the better their essays are likely to be.

Note makers

Give your pupils a pro forma that structures the notes you want them to capture from the debate (for example: "Most persuasive argument?" "Key facts?" "Best attacks?"). They will end the debate with curriculum-based notes and an excellent revision resource.

Active audience

If the culture of your school allows it—and you know that your class can focus for sustained periods—then there is much to be said for allowing your audience to be just that: an audience. Twenty minutes of being engaged in active listening is a productive use of your pupils' time. You will be able to tell if they are listening by allowing them to respond (with "Hear, hear" or "Shame" or through applause) and by noting the questions that they ask during the floor debate.

Assessing the debate

There are many ways of assessing a debate. All that matters is that the particular assessment criteria that are used meet your objectives and that the pupils know them before they stage the debate. There is an off-the-peg set of assessment criteria included in the Appendix F to this book. It equally rewards your pupils' command of content, response, organisation and style. While you may be happy to use this as published, you might instead choose to alter the apportionment of marks: for example, a science teacher may want to allot 80% for content and response and only 20% for style and organisation.

When is the best time to hold a debate?

The most obvious point to hold a debate is at the end of a unit or section of work so as to bring together the knowledge and understanding that the pupils have gained through recent lessons. Debates are also extremely effective when used in revision lessons.

Debates can also be used to introduce a topic and ignite the class's interest, but you will need to give more time and/or resources for research and preparation.

In language lessons, including English, where the objective of the debate is to help the pupils master the skills that are embedded in the subject more than its content, debates can be deployed at any time. Indeed, a lighthearted debate can be an excellent way to mark the end of term. "This house would get rid of Father Christmas" is a more productive activity than showing a video.

One of the advantages of debates is that they take very little planning and can be marked in real time, without compromising any pedagogical value. As a result, busy teachers can plan to use them with a mind to their own workload, running them with younger classes at times of the year when they face a heavy marking load from their examination classes.

Variations, adaptations and notes

If you would like to link the activity more explicitly to the kinds of debates that happen in Parliament, then label the two sides the Government and the Opposition. The speakers are then referred to as follows:

Prime Minister
Deputy Prime Minister
Honourable Member for the Government or Minister of X (if you have more than three speakers)
Government Whip (for the summary speaker)
Leader of the Opposition
Deputy Leader of the Opposition
Honourable Member for the Opposition or Shadow Minister of X
Opposition Whip

The chairperson of the debate will become the Speaker of the House. To render the experience even more authentic, the House could be called upon to divide—"Ayes to the left, noes to the right"—for the vote.

The audience debate (or the "floor debate") is traditionally reserved for the members of the audience, with no opportunity for the main speakers to respond until the summary speakers. However, this session could be replaced by a question-and-answer session.

We recommend that, when introducing debates, only speakers on the opposing team be allowed to offer POIs, but with a more experienced class, this can be opened up so that any member the audience may offer a POI, just as happens in Parliament or in the chambers of the Oxford and Cambridge Unions.

Some teachers like the atmosphere of a noisy debate and permit/encourage the use of "Hear, hear" and "Shame". Others prefer silence. Make sure you brief your audience and indeed your chairperson, who will be in charge of order during the debate. An alternative can be issuing cards saying "Agree" and "Disagree" to the pupils, who are then allowed to hold them up to show their reaction to points made in the debate.

If a debate has been time-set or place-set (for example, one in which the debaters are imagined to be the General Staff during the World War II where the topic is "Should we use mustard gas?"), then costumes or props can be used to add a theatrical element. However, we do not recommend the use of visual aids in general in debates. The speakers should be compelled to use their words alone to explain and persuade—the use of props and exhibits can detract from the focus on oracy.

It can be effective to stage your debate in a larger space; in front of other, perhaps younger, classes; or in an assembly if the topic is suitable.

For a list of suggested topics, see Appendix G.

7 Other forms of debate

Introduction

A Parliamentary Debate is not always the most suitable format for your needs. You might want a shorter format or one that allows more students to speak, one that allows multiple perspectives to be put forward more easily or one that pits individuals against each other. Or you may just want a variety of formats in your toolbox so as to keep your students on their toes and to add interest to a year-long scheme of work. There follows a list of alternative formats which you might consider.

Balloon Debate

Balloon Debates have long since been an end-of-term favourite for English teachers. They work well in this context, but they can have wider pedagogical use too. The concept of these debates rests on the conceit that various people are together on a hot-air balloon that is starting to sink. The only way to save any of them is to start flinging the others over the side. If they go, their contribution and legacy to the world disappear. The figures (played by students in the class) therefore deliver speeches to their classmates, explaining why they should be saved over the other competing personalities. The class then votes on who goes and who survives.

Instructions

Select the pupils to be in the balloon. Either allot them characters to play or allow them to choose their own. If the purpose is primarily to practice persuasive speaking in a fun activity, then it is fine to allow them to choose their own. Indeed, it can be interesting to watch Bart Simpson, David Beckham and Jesus fight it out! Alternatively, if you are interested in having the students explore particular figures (or indeed concepts or materials—the balloon riders do not have to be human) and evaluate the importance of each, then you will need to assign the roles. The preparation for this kind of debate can happen in groups or as an extension activity or homework. If the content matters, then the provision of resources or, alternatively, the opportunity to research will be important. Once the contributors are ready, give them a set time, and allow them to address the class from the front of the room. This could occur just once, or there could be multiple rounds during which the speakers try to denigrate their competitors' claims as well as trumpet their own.

Possible topics

History: Elizabeth I v Cromwell v Gladstone v Lenin
RE: Jesus v Buddha v Moses v Mohammed
Maths: Different maths functions
Science: Newton v Einstein v Darwin v Pascal; biology v chemistry v physics
DT: Wood v metal v plastic v glass
The arts: Van Gogh v Monet v Picasso v Rothko

Planning and resources

Students and roles must be allocated. Optional are resources for research and props or costumes for the balloon riders. A timer is useful, and a graphic of a balloon on the whiteboard and/or sound effects can add some extra dazzle if you are so minded. If you are assessing the students' contributions, then make sure they know in advance what you are looking for. How many marks for persuasive presentation? Language? Research and use of facts? Compelling arguments?

Notes

A successful balloon debate can be re-created in assembly or in front of a younger class.

Boxing Match Debate

Boxing Match Debates are designed to give extra support to those pupils who need to build their confidence in debating. Those teachers who use this format invariably report well on the experience.

Instructions

Choose your topic, and divide the class into the Blue Corner and the Red Corner. Choose a pupil from each side to come forward to "box". They should have a quick back-and-forth exchange on the topic, and when they are struggling, you should "ring the bell". Send them back to their corners, where their classmates can act as their boxing coaches, motivating them and giving them ideas for what to say in the next round. You could vary this approach by sending out a different pupil for the second round, one who has been prepped by the coaches. Any of the topics that you would routinely use for a Parliamentary Debate can be suitable here, but note that it is unlikely to be explored in as much depth. You may want to keep the topics quite simple whilst your students are learning their trade.

Possible topics

PSCHE: Bullies should be permanently excluded from school
Geography: It is good for a city to host a large sporting event
RE: Religions should not allow divorce
History: The Treaty of Versailles led to World War II
Science: It is worse for your health to be too fat than too thin; vaccinations should be compulsory
English: Lady Macbeth was to blame for the murders

Planning and resources

The topic, team and speakers must be chosen. You will need a bell or other audible signal. Other props such as belts and sashes are optional.

Notes

Some teachers are happy for coaches to clap and cheer during the match. Others prefer silence until the bell is rung. Brief your students on your preferences.

There is a video of this activity at https://www.noisyclassroom.com.

Table Debate

Some teachers worry that in the standard parliamentary format, too many in the class are passive. This approach is a great format for getting everyone very actively involved.

Instructions

Divide the class into groups of four or six. Within their groups, your pupils will need to divide themselves into two sides before choosing a speaking order—you can do this for them if you wish. Give them their topics and some time to prepare. The pupils should follow the preparation steps laid out in Chapter 6 on Parliamentary Debate, and, if you want, they can use the pro forma sheets at https://www.noisyclassroom.com. If using groups of four, the pupils should simply omit the summary speeches. When you are ready to start, you will need to chair and time all of the debates simultaneously. You will invite the first speakers to make their speech of three minutes, and all of them will begin. You may need to talk to them beforehand about speaking loudly enough that their group can hear—but not so loudly that they overwhelm the other speakers. Generally, it is surprising how well this activity works and how much each individual group is likely to concentrate on its debate alone. It is hard to formally assess this activity, but you can circulate and get a taste of everyone's contributions. A class discussion afterwards in which members of each group explain what they thought was the most persuasive argument on each side can help to share the best ideas.

Possible topics

Geography: Nuclear power is the best energy choice
Science: Parents should be allowed to choose the characteristics of their unborn
   children; animal testing should be banned
PSCHE/RE: Abortion should be illegal; euthanasia should be allowed
English: Lizzie Bennet is a feminist character
History: The rise of Hitler can be attributed to Germany's economic problems
In addition, you can use any topic used for Parliamentary Debates, Hat Debates and
   Rebuttal Tennis.

Planning and resources

Groups and topics must be allocated. If Table Debates are used at the end of a unit or as revision, the pupils should have all the information that they need to prepare. If they are being used earlier on, pupils may need argument packs or the time to research.

Notes

For more differentiation, group by ability, and choose a range of motions around the same topic area to provide suitable challenge for all.

   We have taken the name "Table Debates" from the terrific blog, *The Debatifier*. There are some excellent videos of this format in practice on its website, http://argumentcentereducation.com/category/the-debatifier/.

Public Meeting

This format is useful when there are different interest groups that need to be represented.

Instructions

Choose a topic, and divide the class into groups, with each group representing different parties interested in the question. Give them the time and necessary resources to think about their position and to prepare one of their members to give a speech. When ready, call on the speaker from each group to put their position forward to the room. The other members of the group stay in role as they question the speakers. At the end of the debate, a vote is taken.

Possible topics

Geography: The building of a new cinema (groups include the cinema developers, local residents, the closest cinema, the landowner, other businesses that want the land, an environmental group)

RE/PSCHE: Legalising assisted suicide (groups include doctors, terminally ill persons, religious groups, hospices, drug companies)

History: Possible routes for the construction of a new railway line during the Industrial Revolution (groups include local residents, factory owners, farmers, railway workers, landowners)

Planning and resources

The groups and the topic must be allocated. Materials to help preparation may be necessary. Optional extras include showing the pupils a speech from a town hall meeting and providing a podium/lectern from which the pupils speak.

Notes

This activity can work well in a space larger than a classroom. It could be arranged across a year group, with each class preparing one perspective and everyone gathering in a hall for the meeting.

Conscience Alley

This activity is suitable when you want your class to make a decision. It is traditionally used when there is a moral dilemma for the pupils to resolve (hence the name). However, there is no reason why it shouldn't be used to make more practical decisions too.

Instructions

Ask your class to form two lines opposite each other. A selected pupil walks slowly down the alley in the middle. As they walk, the pupils on each side try to persuade them to come over to their side. This can be imagined as angels and demons on the shoulder, trying to help the ambulator make a moral decision. If they succeed, the ambulator will take a step towards that row. This can also be used to give the pros and cons for a more practical course of action. You can walk down the alley instead of a student if you wish.

Possible topics

English: Should Hamlet avenge his father? Should Macbeth murder Duncan? Should Willy Loman kill himself?

History: Should Chamberlain pursue appeasement? Should Churchill use disinformation as wartime propaganda?

RE: Should a potential disciple leave their life to follow Jesus?

PE: Which formation should a football team play in?

PSCHE: Should I spend my money or save it?

Planning and resources

Very little is needed beyond choosing a topic. Make sure this activity is physically possible in the space you have.

Notes

This activity can be done in groups instead of as a whole class. In this case, participants can have more than one chance to persuade the undecided, and it can be done seated if space is a problem. This activity works well as a starter to introduce a question before you look at it in more detail.

8 Shorter activities

Introduction

Some of the activities described so far are not for everyday classroom use. An English teacher may run a formal debating unit only once every half term and a science teacher only once a year.

However, the activities presented in this chapter require almost no planning and can be used in your classroom every day and across every subject. The most natural place for them is as starters or plenaries, but they can also be used as transition exercises, extension activities or part of the main body of a lesson. They can all be done in five minutes or less. Even the most reluctant teachers can normally be convinced to incorporate at least one of these activities into their teaching.

Rebuttal Tennis

This is a noisy classroom favourite and can be used with all years, ability levels and subjects. It is a super starter or plenary activity and can be used as a substitute for many other Talk Partner activities. Its main advantage is that it ensures that different perspectives are examined by all pupils. It gives both students in the pair a role, thereby ensuring that turns are taken. Furthermore, it develops critical thinking and listening skills.

Instructions

Put the class in pairs, and in their pairs, have the pupils decide which of them will be Pupil A and which Pupil B. Give Pupil A a debatable statement to "serve"—for example, "The monarchy should be abolished". Pupil A must serve the argument over an imaginary net to their partner by supporting the statement with a reason. When the pupil has finished, he or she gestures hitting the "ball" over the "net". This action ensures that the partner pupil will not interrupt before the reason has been given. Pupil B then "hits" the argument back by listening and disagreeing with that which Pupil A has said. The two pupils continue their rally until they run out of ideas or you halt the exercise. As a small modification, this activity can also be done with one pair at the front of the class. The rest of the class can be asked to act as umpires—waiting too long to respond could be a missed ball, and accidentally arguing on the wrong side could be an "out". Topics can derive from a wide variety of places: anything from the interpretations of sources through to differing methods for answering examination questions.

Possible topics

Maths: Two ways to solve a problem.

Science: Two ways to design an experiment; pros and cons of stem cell research; The UK should abandon nuclear energy.

History: Civil disobedience works; World War I is the main reason why women got the vote.

RE: Competing proofs for the existence of God.

Geography: Tourism harms the developing world; The West should be responsible for dealing with climate change.

English: Othello's tragedy comes from his outsider status; Willie Loman is a good father.

PSCHE: 12-year-olds should be given the vote.

Planning and resources

No planning or resources are needed.

Notes

A video of the activity in practice is available at www.noisyclassroom.com. This approach produces much more focused and critical discussion than just using talk partners.

I Couldn't Disagree More

Instructions

Write statements on the board for the whole class to respond to, or, alternatively, Pitch, Pause, Pounce as part of exposition and whole-class discussion. The only rule is that pupils must begin their answers with the phrase "I couldn't disagree more". For a change, allow the pupils to challenge you.

Possible statements

Maths: This equation would be best solved by x.
PE: The best move next is x.
Science: Nutrition is the most important thing for keeping healthy.
English: The language shows that article x is more biased than article y.
Economics: This data shows x.
History: Violent protest is needed to secure civil rights.

Planning and resources

Selecting your statements is all that is necessary.

Notes

This is a super way to replace closed questions with exchanges that are open and encourage critical thinking.

Where Do You Stand?

Instructions

This whole-class activity works well as a starter or plenary. Label one side of the classroom "Strongly agree" and one side "Strongly disagree". Give the class a statement, and get the pupils to stand at a place along a line from one side to the other that corresponds with how strongly they agree or disagree (the centre of the room can be counted as undecided or neutral territory). Once your pupils are in position, they can discuss their reasons with their neighbours, or you can choose some of them to explain why they have stood in their chosen spot.

Possible statements

English: Studying Shakespeare is a waste of time.
Science: Parents should be allowed to choose their babies' characteristics in the womb.
Computer science: The internet has made the world a better place.
Health and social care: Your manner with the patient is as important as the medicine.
The arts: The best art shocks.
Citizenship: Sixteen- and seventeen-year-olds should be allowed to vote.

Planning and resources

All you need to do is select the statements. Signs saying "Strongly agree" and "Strongly disagree" are optional.

Notes

If your classroom won't easily allow for the free movement of pupils, then tweak the approach to a more binary one: Stand Up for What You Believe In. Ask students who agree with the statement to stand up and those who disagree to stay seated.

Hat Debate

Instructions

Every teacher can have a hat (or box) on their desk that contains topics written on slips of paper. The tasks written on these slips can be used as extension activities or for the whole class if a lesson finishes early or if a change of pace is needed. Form tutors might also have a hat with general topics for consideration during tutor periods. In some subjects, these tasks can be adapted from past examination papers. A topic is picked out of the hat, and students are given a brief time to prepare one side of the argument before facing off against the other side. A pair could do this at the front of the class, or the whole class could do this in pairs or groups. Alternatively, the topics can be used for whole-class spontaneous debates led by the teacher.

Possible topics

History: The rise of the Labour Party was the main reason for the decline of the Liberal Party
RE: The Catholic Church should allow female bishops
Politics: Pressure groups harm democracy
Economics: The government should tax and spend more
Geography: Child labour can be justified in developing countries
Science: Scientists are ethically responsible for the consequences of their work
PSCHE: Under-16s should not have their own mobile phones

Planning and resources

You will need a hat or other container and slips of paper, each with a topic written on it.

Notes

If a teacher wants to start with only one activity in this book, then this is the best one to go for.

9 In character

There are opportunities for students to assume the role of characters in most curricular subjects. Introducing this dramatic element into the classroom is an engaging way of helping students to explore differing perspectives, understand the importance of context and develop empathy and understanding. There is no need for costume—or indeed for changed voices or gesture—but these can add to the impact. And, of course, there is always the opportunity for the teacher to get involved as well!

Hot Seating

Instructions

This is a favourite activity of many English teachers. They place pupils in the shoes of literary characters, but the same approach can be applied broadly across the curriculum. A pupil (or the teacher) takes on a role and sits in the hot seat so as to be questioned by the rest of the class. The activity can be effective for seeing different perspectives, understanding context and building empathy. Pupils should be given the chance to prepare questions (individually or in pairs), and, unless the character is very familiar, the one who takes the hot seat will also need time and materials to prepare. The activity can be made even more engaging by using costumes or props or by "performing" the role (if the pupil or teacher is willing and able), but these adornments are not necessary for the critical thinking to take place. Historical figures, scientists, economists, religious leaders and artists are all good candidates for taking the hot seat.

Possible figures

English: Ralph, Scrooge, Jane Eyre, Caliban, Mickey Johnstone, Shakespeare, Austen
History: Chamberlain, Stalin, Gandhi, Martin Luther King Jr, Lloyd George, Emmeline Pankhurst

Science: Einstein, Newton, Darwin, Oppenheimer, Marie Curie
Economics: Keynes, Adam Smith, Milton Friedman, Marx, Amartya Sen
RE: Moses, Buddha, the Pope, Paul
The arts: Picasso, Brecht, Philip Glass
Languages: Anybody speaking the mother tongue!

Planning and resources

Pupils may need time and materials to prepare depending on their prior knowledge of character and the context. Optional costumes and props add to the fun.

Mock Trial

Instructions

Mock Trials can be elaborate set-piece activities involving a lot of planning and class time. However, adapted formats can be more easily fitted into a scheme of work. The premise is that your literary character, scientist, town planner or historical figure has been charged with a crime and the class must use evidence and interrogation to reach a verdict. This format allows the class to consider contradictory evidence, examine differing perspectives and appreciate the complexity of the issue. When using the whole exercise, everyone in the class will need to be assigned a role (lawyer or lawyer's team, witness, defendant, court staff, judge or jury). Everyone will need briefing on their role, and the lawyers will need to be provided with evidence packs or the time to do research themselves (some ready-made resource packs for Mock Trials can be found on the internet). Once everyone is prepared, the judge will preside and follow a timetable of calling on the lawyers to make statements, call witnesses, cross-examine and conclude. The jury will then make its decision. There is inbuilt differentiation in this activity. A scaled-down version of this, which would take less class time, would be to have a smaller group prepare the trial as an extension activity, with the rest of the class then acting as the jury.

Possible figures

English: Macbeth, anyone from *An Inspector Calls*, Juliet's parents, Gatsby, Henry
   V, Frankenstein
History: Henry VIII, Chamberlain, Field Marshall Haig
Science: Oppenheimer, an animal tester, a genetic engineer
PE: Lance Armstrong
RE: Savonarola

Planning and resources

This activity can be demanding in terms of preparation, with lots of resources needing to be produced (or acquired). Pupils need briefing sheets on their different roles and may need evidence packs, witness statements etc. Such resources can be enormous fun to produce and can then be used by all classes for many years to justify the effort. You may also want to provide costumes and props to make the activity even more special. The pupils will need class time to prepare in advance of the trial. The room will need to be arranged as a courtroom with desks for the lawyers, a witness box, a judge's table (with a gavel, ideally), jury benches and a dock for the accused.

Notes

This can also be a good activity to do with a subject-based club or as an off-timetable day activity (where the planning and trial all happen in one day). The activity is an effective way of affirming understanding of the legal system gained in PSCHE.

For enthusiastic pupils, there are national mock trial competitions that your school could enter.

Question Time

Instructions

Have you ever fancied yourself as David Dimbleby? Here is your chance. This is a more dynamic version of hot seating. Choose four pupils to take on related roles on the panel, with the rest of the class as the audience (you can also have a pupil chairperson if you wish, though this is a more challenging role than it looks). Give everyone a chance to prepare questions and research their character if necessary. Then let the fun begin. Passing around a handheld microphone can help with turn taking and authenticity even if it isn't turned on. For additional fireworks, brief some members of the audience for passionate outbursts!

Possible figures

History: Figures around women's suffrage in 1910, appeasement in 1938 or civil rights in the 1960s

Geography: Figures around globalisation, the environment or a specific local issue

Economics: Figures around the financial crash in 2008

English: The main characters in any text studied

Science: Different figures concerned with genetic science (scientist, religious figure, doctor, ethical philosopher), animal testing, nuclear energy or space travel

Planning and resources

You will need to assign roles and provide any research materials needed. Preparing to be a panelist is an excellent extension activity for more able students. Your classroom will need to be set up with the panel at the front. The microphone is optional. You may want to show a clip of the show in advance so as to familiarise the pupils with the format.

Chat Show

Instructions

Think Jerry Springer or Jeremy Kyle. This activity is guaranteed to give you a noisy classroom—so give appropriate notice to neighbours or, ideally, book a drama space. You or a very capable pupil takes the role of a chat show host in order to deal with a sticky issue that only this format can properly unravel. Pupils are assigned characters to be called onto the stage at the appropriate moments, while the rest of the class gets authentically into role as the outraged audience, ready to comment with passion and anger. Shakespeare plays lend themselves very well to this format: "He killed my father and married my mother." "She dressed up like a boy and pretended to be a servant so she could get close to the man she loved."

Possible topics

English: *Romeo and Juliet*, *Hamlet* or almost any Shakespeare play; *Blood Brothers*;
    Pride and Prejudice; *Lord of the Flies*
History: The court of Henry VIII
Politics: Characters in any scandal, such as Profumo affair; Donald Trump

Planning and resources

You will need to assign characters and provide the necessary time and/or materials to prepare. Costumes and props are optional but fun extras. It may be worth showing a (carefully chosen) clip of the show in advance.

News Broadcast

This activity is an effective way of focussing knowledge and opinion around a notable event or discovery. It provides plenty of opportunity for differentiation and great fun.

Instructions

In groups, pupils are given one or more events to report as a news broadcast. They must act as anchors, roving journalists, key characters, witnesses, experts and any other relevant interviewees. Give the groups time to plan, script and rehearse, and then allow them to show their broadcasts to the rest of the class. If you have the ability to have the groups film the broadcasts and share them digitally, all the better—of course, paying due attention to your school's safeguarding policies. If not, a cut-out rectangle held in front of whoever is currently "on air" will do the trick perfectly well.

Possible topics

History: The execution of Anne Boleyn
Science: The discovery of penicillin or DNA
Geography: The Mexico earthquake
English: The death of Willy Loman
RE: The Resurrection
PSCHE: Mental health issues affecting teenagers

Planning and resources

You will need to allocate the groups and the topics. As for the roles within the groups, you can assign them or allow the pupils to decide. You will also need to provide any research material the groups need to prepare the content of their broadcasts. Filming equipment or a "TV frame" is optional. You could also show the class a well-chosen news broadcast before they embark on their own.

Notes

If your school has a Media Studies Department, you could run this as a joint project.

10 Structures for critical group or whole-class work

Most classrooms will at least occasionally entertain whole-class discussions and/or group-work activities. These activities can give structure, focus and fun to class talk.

On That Point (or Please Interrupt Me!)

Instructions

This is an excellent activity for practising active, critical listening and for exploring multiple perspectives. In the parliamentary debate format, there is a facility to interrupt the person speaking called a "point of information". The person who wishes to interrupt a speech will rise to their feet and say, "On a point of information". He or she will then wait to hear whether the speaker will accept or decline the point. If accepted, the person interrupting poses a short question or counterargument to the speaker and then sits down, thereby allowing the speaker the floor once again. In this activity, the teacher or a confident student begins to give a speech on a controversial topic. The rest of the class must stand to offer points of information as the speech goes on. The rules can vary. The speaker can be compelled to accept all the points or may be allowed to refuse some to get thorough some of their speech. It can be compulsory or optional for every pupil in the class to offer a point. Pupils can be limited to one point or be allowed multiple interruptions. The speech can be time-limited or not.

Possible topics

RE: The Church of England should not remarry divorcees
Geography: Nuclear power is the most environmentally friendly means of producing energy
PE: All sport should be played in unisex teams

Politics: The British prime minister can exercise more power than the American president

Science: Human cloning should be allowed

Planning and resources

You will need to think about your speech if you are in the hot seat (but be prepared to have to abandon it once the points come flying!). A stopwatch will be needed if timing.

Notes

The speaker will feel under considerable pressure. After all, it might be 25 against 1 or some such. If you have been brave enough to try, remember it is a game, and try not to get flustered. In most classes, there are likely to be pupils begging to have a go at being the speaker after you have modelled it once. However, there is sometimes more pedagogical value in your controlling the narrative. When delivering workshops in schools, this is one of the most popular activities that we run.

Dragon's Den

Instructions

Based on the famous television show where entrepreneurs pitch ideas to ferocious investors in the *Dragon's Den*, this group-work activity forces pupils to justify their ideas. In groups, pupils work on a pitch. It doesn't have to be a business idea, though, of course, it can certainly work in a business studies lesson. It can also be a strategy to avoid or end a war in history, an interpretation of a poem in English literature or a foreign aid plan in geography. The key feature of this format is that the group must prepare a short presentation and then be ready to be grilled on its details by "the dragons". These people could be played by yourself and able pupils. A nice added extra is to invite older pupils, other members of staff, members of senior management or outside guests to be the dragons. This helps to replicate the feeling of pressure in presenting to strangers or to senior figures that many pupils will likely face in their working lives.

Possible pitches

History: Giving independence to Ireland in 1918

PE: Making a significant rule change in rugby

Theatre studies: Always performing Shakespeare in period costume/context

RE: Persuading the Catholic Church to endorse contraception

Economics: Cutting taxes to promote economic growth

Planning and resources

You will need to select groups and topics (or allow the groups to choose their own) and appoint dragons. It can be useful to hold the pitches somewhere other than the classroom, but it is not a necessity.

Notes

This is an excellent revision activity, where different groups can cover various aspects of the syllabus.

Fishbowl Discussion

This is a form of observed group work that allows for peer learning.

Instructions

A group of pupils forms an inner circle and has a group discussion on the directed topic. The other pupils form an outer circle, observe the group and take notes (either free notes or on a worksheet). In some adaptations, the outer circle may question the inner circle at the end. This can be rotated so that everyone has a turn in the centre, or it can be used to allow the modelling of effective group discussion or the dissemination of ideas from an extension group to the rest of the class.

Possible topics

History: What were the main causes of World War II?
Science: What would be the best way to set up this experiment?
Geography: What effects can development aid have on a country?
Drama: How can we convey the emotional message of the scene?
English: What bias can we find in the newspaper articles?

Planning and resources

You will need to allocate the groups and topics. Preparation of worksheets for outer circle to complete is optional.

Notes

This can be useful for revision, where groups concentrate on different questions and then share their thinking.

Expert Groups

This is an active, cooperative, pupil-led activity that can last over a number of lessons.

Instructions

Pupils should be divided into groups of four to six, and each group should be given a topic, question or task to master so as to build "expert" knowledge and understanding. The group members will need the necessary time, materials, research opportunities and support to build their expertise as necessary. When this period is finished, the class should regroup with new groups, each one having one member of one of the expert groups. This "expert" will teach the other pupils in their group what they have mastered and face questions on it.

Possible topics

Politics: A particular election, Supreme Court judgement or political figure
The arts: One artist, school or technique
English: One short story or poem from an anthology
ICT: One programming function
Science: One experiment
Maths: One problem or approach to solution

Planning and resources

You will need to allocate the groups and topics. Also consider whether the groups need materials, access to computers or the library for research or homework time to prepare?

Notes

In mixed-ability groups, this activity can be differentiated by task. This can be useful for revision lessons, where different groups are assigned units on which to focus.

Argument Stations

This is based on an activity created by Argument-Centered Education, an organization that was founded by argument literacy expert Les Lynn. It can be found on *The Debatifier*, a thought-leading blog in the field. It is a fantastic way to stretch more able pupils and get them to examine multiple interpretations and approaches.

Instructions

Pick between one and four pupils to represent a particular interpretation of a text or approach to a question, and have anywhere between two and five positions represented around the classroom. Give the pupils the opportunity to research their position so that they feel comfortable defending it. In a mixed-ability class, stretch your most able pupils by giving them the most challenging positions. When the pupils are ready, they should stand at their argument station, ready to explain, expand on and defend their interpretation. The rest of the class should be given different extracts from texts or problems to solve, perhaps in pairs, and they should have the chance to read and digest their material. They should then visit the stations in turn; the representatives at each one will look at their material and argue why it supports their view. In English lessons, this may involve the consideration of different extracts from the core text; in history lessons, it might be different primary or secondary sources, with the stations presenting different critical viewpoints. In lessons about maths, science, politics or economics, the wanderers may have problems to solve, and the stations can represent different functions, experiments, parties' policies or approaches. The wanderers should have worksheets to fill in to record what they learn as they circulate around the room. Opportunities should be given for pupils to share and discuss the ideas that have been generated through the activity.

Possible topics

English: The reason for Othello's tragedy: His outsider status v the incompatibility of soldier and lover v Iago's skill as a manipulator (Wanderers have different extracts from the play.)

History: The reason for the rise of the Labour Party: The decline of the Liberal Party v the extension of the franchise v the strengthening of the trades unions (Wanderers have primary and secondary sources.)

Science: How to approach a particular experiment; how to solve the energy crisis (The stations are different solutions, and the wanderers have different roles— e.g. government, business, individual, environmentalist.)

Maths: How to approach a particular maths problem (Wanderers have problems to try out.)

Geography: Which of these projects should receive our foreign aid? (Wanderers have success criteria.)

Politics: Which political party should you vote for: Conservatives v Labour v Liberal Democrats v Green v UKIP? (Wanderers have different policy areas—e.g. employment, environment, education.)

Citizenship: What is the best way to effect political change: Protest march v letters and petitions v civil disobedience v insider lobbying? (Wanderers have different changes they wish to make—from very local ones like the construction of a new skate park through to global issues like climate change.)

Planning and resources

This activity needs careful planning. Pupils need to be allocated to different argument stations and will need the materials or opportunity to research to be able to defend their positions. The remaining pupils need to be assigned differentiated sheets with text to interpret or problems to solve, and they also need a worksheet to record the information you want them to elicit. With an advanced class that has done this activity before, you may be able to allow pupils to self-select positions and extracts/problems, with guidance, as part of the learning process.

Notes

There is a resourced example of this activity that uses interpretations of *Catcher in the Rye* on *The Debatifier* website.

It is easy to run a simpler version of this activity in which the majority of pupils simply visit the stations (without a particular source or problem). The pupils who are manning the stations then try to persuade them generally of their position. Such an approach can be easily set up when a class is planning for an essay question, choosing a format for an experiment or solving a moral dilemma.

Formats for critical pair discussion

Talk Partners and Think-Pair-Share are common strategies in classrooms today. However, there are other formats that can be used to encourage depth and breadth in conversation and to kick-start critical thinking.

Teacher-Pupil Pairs

This activity allows pupils the chance for extended speaking and extended listening and can help them to clarify and explain their ideas.

Instructions

Put the class into pairs, and allot to each pupil in the pair the role of either Pupil A or Pupil B. Ask a question, and get Pupil A to teach Pupil B the answer whilst Pupil B listens and makes notes. Some Bs can then be called on to report back what they have learnt to the class. Swap roles with a different question.

Possible questions

English: What descriptive devices does the poet use in this poem?
Science: How does the respiratory process work?
RE: What happens in this parable, and what does it mean?
Maths: How do you solve this equation?
ICT: How do you sort and filter on Excel?

Planning and resources

Choosing the questions is all that is necessary.

Rotating Circles

This activity allows pupils to work with a number of different talk partners and can be used in conjunction with Rebuttal Tennis, Teacher-Pupil Pairs or a simple Think-Pair-Share approach.

Instructions

Set up the chairs in the classroom in an inner and an outer circle with the chairs facing each other or in lines with the chairs facing each other, as your space allows. Set your pair activity, but when the bell rings, one line of pupils gets up and moves one space to the next partner. One might see this as the speed-dating approaching to pair work!

Possible topics

These topics are suitable for any subject:
   What do you already know about x? (to introduce a topic)
   What would you like to find out about z? (to introduce a topic)
   What do you remember about y? (to revisit a topic)
   How would you approach this exam question/essay/task?
   What were the key features/points about x? (as a plenary)
See Rebuttal Tennis for debatable topics.

Planning and resources

You will need to set up the classroom and select the topics for discussion. This activity can be useful as a starter if, before the class's arrival, you have already configured the classroom.

Quiz and Switch

This activity gets pupils out of their seats and moving around as they ask and answer each other's questions. It works especially well as a starter activity.

Instructions

Give your pupils notecards with questions written on them. They could each have a different question, or there could be duplicates. The pupils set off around the room so as to find a partner to ask their question. They then answer their partner's question, switch their cards and set off to find a new partner.

Possible questions

PSCHE: What do you believe about marriage/living together/divorce?
Maths: How do you solve this problem? (using any problem!)
English: How do you define this technical word? (e.g. onomatopoeia, alliteration, metaphor)
History: Can you give me three facts about this historical figure?
Science: Can you explain this process? (e.g. photosynthesis, osmosis, electrolysis)

Planning and resources

You will need to prepare the notecards given to the pupils in advance (or they could be given blank notecards and write their own questions).

Question and Answer Pair-Up

Instructions

This is similar to Quiz and Switch, but this time half of the cards have the answers to the questions that the other half pose. Pupils receive, read and reflect on their cards. They then begin to move around the room, locating their other half. Once they are in pairs, the questions and answers can be read to the room to be verified and discussed.

Possible questions

English literature: "Who said?": a quotation and the character/speaker's name
History: "What happened on this date?": events and their dates
Maths: Problems "What's the answer?": problems and their answers
Science: "What does it represent?": elements and their chemical symbol; "How does it work?": key processes and their explanations
PE: "What do they do?": positions and a description of their role
ICT: "What's their function?" keys and a description of their function

Planning and resources

You will need to prepare the notecards with questions and answers in advance of their first use, but they can be reused thereafter.

Notes

The cards can be differentiated if they are to be used in mixed-ability groups. The questions on cards can be duplicated several times, or they can all be unique.

12 Activities to build oracy skills

These activities are designed to allow students explicitly to practice their oracy skills. Unlike the other activities in this book, they will not aid the teaching of the wider curriculum and will most likely be used in the English classroom, in tutor time or in other designated slots for building communication skills. With the exception of How Are You Feeling? they would also work well in a Modern Foreign Languages or English as an additional language setting because they all get pupils talking.

The Um-er Game

This activity encourages fluency of speech. Although traditionally "um" and "er" are usually chosen as the "banned words", you could come up with your own list, which might include "like", "you know", "innit" or any other fillers that you want your students to avoid.

Instructions

Divide class into groups (of approximately eight pupils), with two teams within each group. Each team writes down topics for speeches on slips of paper. Students then take turns speaking for 60 seconds on the topic they pick (blindly) from the other team's suggestions, without saying "um" or "er" (or any other words on your banned list). The maximum number of points that they can earn for their team is 60 (60 seconds with no points deducted for banned words). If they speak for 43 seconds with 7 "ums" and "ers", then their score is 36. The other team must listen very closely to pick up on every point lost.

Possible topics

Football
Reality television

The weather
The environment
Fashion magazines
Pets
While you can suggest topics such as these, it is often best to get teams to come up with their own.

Planning and resources

You will need stopwatches for timing the speeches.

Notes

You could bring one student to the front of the class to play this game while the whole class counts the "ums". A harder adaptation of this game is to play Just a Minute: as in the radio show of the same name, the students must avoid not only hesitation but also repetition and deviation.

Defend the Indefensible

By coming up with crazy propositions, students can think about the techniques of persuasion rather than the content.

Instructions

Have a bank of indefensible topics (for example, this house would mandate that all men over 21 wear a beret in public at times), or get the students to generate their own. In groups or with individuals standing at the front of the class, students select a topic and have a few moments to prepare a one-minute speech that seeks to persuade their peers of their position (it can work to have the next student prepare whilst one is speaking so as to keep things moving).

After each speech, get the group/class to identify the persuasive techniques that were used and to record these tactics until you have a large bank of them at the end. Encourage students to look for language, voice, facial expressions, body language, rhetorical devices, use of example/analogy etc.

Possible topics

1. Teachers' salaries should be paid in peppermints

2. Toddlers should decide their parents' bedtimes

3. It should be against the law not to answer the telephone when it rings

4. Politicians should always wear clown suits to official duties

5. Left-handed people should get two votes in general elections

Have fun coming up with your own—the sillier the better!

Planning and resources

You will just need to provide the topics unless you want the students to generate their own.

Notes

You could also do this activity in the form of a written exercise, or you could bring in visual forms of persuasion such as posters. Groups could make promotional videos for their positions, or they could write their positions up as biased or sensationalised newspaper articles.

Giving and Following Instructions

This is an exercise in precise and accurate speaking and close listening.

Instructions

This activity works best if you do it first as a whole class and then divide into pairs. Send one student out of the class (or step outside yourself) while the class decides on a simple object for the "artist" to draw (house, teddy bear, flower etc.). When the student comes back in, the class must give them instructions to draw the object on the board, without them knowing what they are drawing. They will quickly get the idea that "Draw a straight line" is not enough. "Draw a vertical straight line in the middle of the board about 20 cm long" might give them a better chance. It is important for the "artist" to just follow the instructions exactly as given, even if they work out what they think they are drawing.

Planning and resources

No planning is needed. A board with pens and a board wiper is needed for the whole-class version. Paper and pens are fine to play this in pairs.

Notes

A plenary after the exercise can draw out the features of good instruction giving and the importance of precise language generally.

How Are You Feeling?

By removing language from the game, students concentrate on body language, facial expressions and use of voice as means of communication.

Instructions

In groups or as a whole class, individual students pick an emotion from a list and act it out for the others to guess. The trick is that they are not allowed to use any words apart from an agreed-upon phrase. This is often done with "mamamoo" as the permitted word (and this does seem to produce much hilarity). I have also heard of it being done with nothing but the word "banana" or with a quotation from a text. You can pick one of these, choose your own or allow the class to decide. Using nothing but that word or phrase, the speaker must adapt their voice, face and body to allow the audience to guess their emotion.

Possible emotions

Scared
Angry
Surprised
Happy
Disappointed
Nervous
Embarrassed
Arrogant
Shocked
Excited
Overjoyed

Resources and planning

No planning or resources are needed.

Notes

You can move on from emotions to situations to make it more advanced. They could include the following:
    Saying I'm sorry
    Saying I love you/proposing
    Asking for directions
    Reading the weather

Giving an assembly
Telling a joke

Expand-Contract

This exercise helps students think about developing points in more detail and also about getting to the point in a more concise way.

Instructions

This exercise works well in pairs, but it is worth modelling in front of the class first. Give the speaker a point to make. This could be linked to the curriculum or be any single argument for any topic. Give them 30 seconds to make their argument. Next tell them to make the same argument but for one minute, thus forcing them to go into more depth. Finally, tell them to make the argument for a third time in just 15 seconds, thus forcing them to use concise language to get to the heart of the issue.

Possible points

1. Homework puts students under too much pressure.

2. Mobile phones could help with in-class research.

3. Violent video games make people more violent.

4. Giving police guns would act as a deterrent to crime.

5. Having a monarchy is undemocratic.

Notes

You can change these timings to add or reduce the challenge for your students. This is an exercise all trainee teachers should have to go through too! When choosing your topic, make sure that it is a single point and not a whole proposition—after all, we are looking at expanding and condensing the reasoning, not simply increasing the number of points that are made to support the position.

Appendices

Appendix A: The Noisy Manifesto

As toddlers, we learn to speak by listening to those around us. Speaking and listening are essential throughout our education, whether the learning outcome is reading or writing, science or history, a target-led GCSE examination or a freewheeling creative work. The workplaces of tomorrow will be based as much on face-to-face discussions, Skype calls and videos as on traditional reading and writing—so pencils down and ears open for our Noisy Manifesto.

1. A noisy classroom can be a sign of engaged pupils who are active in their learning.

2. Silence is important for reading, writing and reflection, but it is not always the golden rule. Debate, discussion and dialogue are vital too.

3. Teachers are always in control of the decibel levels—the classroom is noisy only when they want it to be.

4. Not everyone can always make noise at the same time; teaching good listening skills is at the heart of the noisy classroom.

5. If we want to send off confident and articulate young adults into the world, we must let them practise their spoken skills as well as their reading and writing.

6. Please be considerate of your neighbours. Warn them in advance of a noisy lesson, or try to book another space in the school.

7. Please be open-minded to noise. Don't assume that a noisy classroom is out of control—it could be where the most exciting learning in the school is going on.

Appendix B: Key vocabulary for debates

Motion or resolution	The topic that is to be debated. In many formats, this is phrased "This house...", in reference to legislative houses.
Proposition or affirmative or government	The side that agrees with the motion.
Opposition or negative	The side that disagrees with the motion.
Chairperson or speaker or moderator	The person in charge of the debate who makes sure that everyone follows the rules and who introduces the speakers.
Timekeeper	The person who keeps time and gives time signals.
Point of information	A structured way of interrupting a speaker.
Rebuttal or refutation	The response made to the argument on the other side.
Floor debate	A period during or after the debate when the audience members can share their views.
Summary speech or reply speech	The final speech in each side that sums up the key issues in the debate.
Protected time	The period at the start and end of a speech when no points of information can be offered.
Accepted/taken/rejected/declined	Words used by the speaker when offered a point of information to show whether they will allow the interruption.
Burden of proof	What the team members feels they need to prove in order to win the debate.
Model	The details of the practical implementation of a policy.
Clash	The areas of the debate on which the two sides have disagreed.
Definition	The terms of the debate.
Counterproposal	An alternative plan the opposition puts forward instead of supporting the status quo.

Appendix C: Sentence starters and connectives for critical oracy

Sentence starters

I believe that…

From my point of view/perspective,…

I disagree with you/the speaker because…

I mainly agree but…

I agree and I would like to add that…

Building on what you/the speaker before said,…

One thing I would like to add is…

Do you have any evidence for that?

Could you clarify…?

I am interested in knowing more about…

I'd like to go back to the point about…

What I heard you say is…

Does everybody agree that…?

Does anybody have anything to add to that?

Others have said that…, but I would like to argue that…

It may be true to say…, but you can also argue that…

I would strongly urge you to consider that…

I would like to counter that point by saying…

I cannot accept that point because…

Connectives

Firstly

To begin

Initially

My first point is

Moreover

Additionally

Furthermore

Secondly

Also

Lastly

In summary

Finally

Appendix D: Argument and speech structure

Argument structure

Point

Explanation

Evidence

If you use a variation on this for your essay writing (e.g. Point Evidence Analysis Link), then it makes sense to mirror what they will use in their writing in their speaking.

Following is an example from a debate on nuclear energy. Note: This is a demonstration only. Pupils should not write out full sentences but rather use bullet points from which to speak.

Point: Nuclear energy is bad for human health.

Explanation: Although accidents at nuclear power stations are rare, when they occur, they can be catastrophic because of the radiation that can escape. A problem with a nuclear reactor can cause problems to human health that can last for generations.

Evidence: The worst accident in a nuclear power station was when the reactor at Chernobyl exploded in 1986. After the disaster, there was a threefold increase in birth defects, and the levels of thyroid cancer and other cancers and respiratory diseases showed sharp increases. In 2011, there was a disaster in Japan when the Fukushima reactors were affected by an earthquake. This shows that nuclear power stations can still be dangerous in developed countries in the 21st century.

Speech structure

Rhetorical opening

Introduction

Preview

Definition or rebuttal

Point one

Point two

Point three

Summary

Conclusion

Again, this example relates to a debate on nuclear energy.

Rhetorical opening: Would you want to live next door to a nuclear power station? Would you feel safe?

Introduction: Today I am going to argue that we should ban nuclear energy.

Preview: I have three points to support my position: firstly, that nuclear energy is bad for human health; secondly, that it is bad for the environment; and thirdly, that it is too expensive.

Definition: I define this by saying that governments around the world should not commission any new nuclear power stations and should gradually decommission all those currently being used. They should replace nuclear power with alternative energy sources like wind and solar.

OR

Rebuttal: The opposition has argued that nuclear power is green, but what if there is a disaster? How green is it to leak radiation into the environment?

Point one

> *Point*: Nuclear energy is bad for human health.
> *Explanation*: Although accidents at nuclear power stations are rare, when they occur, they can be catastrophic because of the radiation that can escape. A problem with a nuclear reactor can cause problems to human health that can last for generations.
> *Evidence:* The worst accident in a nuclear power station was when the reactor at Chernobyl exploded in 1986. After the disaster, there was a threefold increase in birth defects, and the levels of thyroid cancer and other cancers and respiratory diseases showed sharp increases. In 2011, there was a disaster in Japan when the Fukushima reactors were affected by an earthquake. This shows that nuclear power stations can still be dangerous in developed countries in the 21st century.

Point two: Point. Explanation. Evidence.

Point three: Point. Explanation. Evidence.

Summary: I have told you why we should ban nuclear energy: it harmful to human health, damaging to the environment and way too expensive.

Conclusion: I therefore ask you to vote for the proposition.

Appendix E: Examples of topic-based vocabulary for pre-teaching

Topic: City centres should be made car-free

Pollution

Transportation

Commercial interests

Emergency vehicles

Respiratory diseases

Greenhouse effect

Fossil fuels

Congestion

Mobility problems

Residents

Zoning

Electric vehicles

Asthma

Greater good

Topic: Violent video games should be banned

Causation/correlation

Active/passive

Moral/immoral

Freedom of choice

Nanny state

Gratuitous violence

Age certification

Parental responsibility

Peer pressure

Immersive

Brainwashing

Desensitisation

Normalisation

Outlet for aggression

Appendix F: Assessment

Assessment will vary for the particular task, pupil age and subject. These sample assessment criteria for a debate weight arguments, responses, style and organisation equally. You can tweak these for debates and other oracy activities in the classroom. For example, you may wish to

■ Change the weighting to give more emphasis to content.

■ Add a section on use of language.

■ Leave out responses if you are marking individual presentations.

■ Leave out structure if the activity is more discussion-based.

The arguments

What's said: the points that are chosen, how well they are analysed and the evidence or illustrations supporting them.

The responses

The listening demonstrated through rebuttal, responses, questions and points of information.

The style

How it's said: the quality of the language used, vocal techniques, body language, eye contact and gesture.

The organisation

Is the speech organised and ordered into points with an introduction and a conclusion? Do speakers use their time well? Do they work as a team?

	1-2	3-4	5-6	7-8	9-10
Arguments	Provides some explanation of least one relevant argument	States at least two relevant arguments and uses limited evidence to support them	Presents well-chosen arguments with some analysis and relevant evidence	Offers carefully selected arguments that are analysed in some depth and supported with well-chosen evidence	Makes persuasive and original arguments that are analysed in depth and supported by pertinent evidence
Responses	Some attempt at interaction is shown through a question/rebuttal/point of information	Some listening is shown through limited rebuttal and/or questions/points of information	Active listening is demonstrated through regular interaction	Critical listening is shown through analytical responses to others	In-depth critical listening is shown through thoughtful and thorough challenges to others
Style	Limited attempts are made to engage the audience with some variety of delivery and language	Eye contact and some vocal variety are used, along with appropriate language choices	Language, voice and body language are varied and used to engage the audience	Delivery and language choice enhance the speech and fully engage the audience	Delivery and language choice work to produce a compelling and memorable speech
Organisation	An introduction and some independent points can be recognised	There is a clear ordering of points with an introduction and conclusion	The speech is clearly structured and signposted and uses the time well	Effective ordering, labelling and timing of points and a strong introduction and conclusion are evident	Originality makes an effectively structured and timed speech more memorable

Appendix G: List of topics for debate and discussion

English language and foreign language teachers can pick from any of these topics.

PSCHE

- Community service is a better punishment than prison for non-violent crimes
- We should introduce a curfew for under-16s
- All police officers should carry guns
- All secondary schools should be co-educational
- The voting age should be lowered to 12 (or 16)
- Queen Elizabeth II should be the last British monarch
- We should ban violent video games
- Assisted suicide should be legalised

Geography

- We should eat only food produced in Britain
- We should ban cars from cities
- Globalisation has marginalised the poor
- We should prioritise tackling climate change over economic growth
- Tourism does less economically developed countries more harm than good

Science

- Scientific testing on animals should be banned
- We support a manned mission to Mars
- Children can make a big difference to the environment
- Parents should be able to choose the genetic characteristics of their children
- Nuclear energy should be banned
- Genetically modified foods should be banned
- Single-use plastics should be banned
- We should all be vegetarians

- We should ban junk food for children

- It is worse to eat too much than to eat too little

PE

- Boxing should be banned

- Competitive sports should not be played in schools

- Sports stars are bad role models for young people

- Every child should join a sports club

- Performance-enhancing drugs should be legalised

- All sport should be mixed-gender

The arts

- This house believes that we shouldn't teach art and music in schools

- Prizes and awards damage the arts more than they help them

- Talent shows like *The X Factor* damage the music industry

- Modern art is not real art

- Good art should have a message

- Plays should always be performed in period costume

- *X* film version of a book or production of a play or recording of a symphony is better than *Y*

Economics

- We should significantly raise taxes to pay for services

- Austerity was the best reaction to the 2008 financial crash

- The richest should pay significantly more tax

- Global sanctions should be used to leverage better human rights

Politics

- The British prime minister can be described as primus inter pares

- Pressure groups are harmful to democracy

- Voting should be compulsory

- Britain should use a proportional representation voting system

- Extreme political parties should be banned
- Political parties should be funded by the state
- The British prime minister has more powers than the US president

History

- The Treaty of Versailles was the main cause of World War II
- The rise of the Labour Party led to the decline of the Liberal Party
- Oliver Cromwell was a great leader
- (time-set in 1913) Women should be given the vote

Literature

- Romeo's and Juliet's parents are to blame for the tragedy
- Willy Loman "had all the wrong dreams"
- The original ending to *Great Expectations* is the superior one
- The tragedy in *Othello* is due to his outsider status
- Henry V is more a war criminal than a hero
- Poets show that the mental suffering of war was worse than the physical
- Friel's *Translations* is about "language and language only"
- In Gilead, women are oppressed by other women more than they are by men

Appendix H: Debate speech scaffold sheets

Printable versions of these can be found at https://www.noisyclassroom.com.

3-a-side debate format

© Noisy Classroom, 2018
noisyclassroom.com

First Proposition notes sheet

Motion	

Definition	What key words or phrases need to be clarified?

	First speaker's points (my points)		Second speaker's points	
Our team's points	1		1	
	2		2	
	3		3	

1	2	3
Name of point:	Name of point:	Name of point:
Develop your point (use a structure like 'Name, Explain, Evidence' or 'Reason, Evidence, Analysis, Link (REAL)'	Develop your point (use a structure like 'Name, Explain, Evidence' or 'Reason, Evidence, Analysis, Link (REAL)'	Develop your point (use a structure like 'Name, Explain, Evidence' or 'Reason, Evidence, Analysis, Link (REAL)'

Conclusion	As well as reminding us of what points you've made, try to end with a strong statement.

3-a-side debate format

the noisy classroom

Notes for 1st Opp, 2nd Prop & 2nd Opp

Motion	

	First speaker's points	Second speaker's points
Our team's points	1	1
	2	2
	3	3

	The other team said ...	But we disagree, because ...
Rebuttal		

1	2	3
Name of point:	Name of point:	Name of point:
Develop your point (use a structure like 'Name, Explain, Evidence' or 'Reason, Evidence, Analysis, Link (REAL)'	Develop your point (use a structure like 'Name, Explain, Evidence' or 'Reason, Evidence, Analysis, Link (REAL)'	Develop your point (use a structure like 'Name, Explain, Evidence' or 'Reason, Evidence, Analysis, Link (REAL)'

Conclusion	As well as reminding us of what points you've made, try to end with a strong statement.

the noisy classroom

3-a-side debate format
Basic summary speech notes sheet

Motion	

	The floor speaker said ...	We agree/disagree, because ...
Points from the floor		

	First speaker's points	Second speaker's points
Our team's points	1	1
	2	2
	3	3

	The other team said ...	But we disagree, because ...
The other team's points	1	
	2	
	3	
	4	
	5	
	6	

Conclusion	As well as reminding us of what points you've made, try to end with a strong statement.

3-a-side debate format

the noisy classroom

Advanced summary speech notes sheet

Motion	

The three most important issues in today's debate were:
1
2
3

	The other team / Floor speakers who disagreed with us said ...	We say ... / Floor speakers who agreed with us said ...
Summary of three key areas	1	
	2	
	3	

Conclusion	As well as reminding us of what points you've made, try to end with a strong statement.

© Noisy Classroom, 2017
noisyclassroom.com

the noisy classroom

3-a-side debate format
Chairperson's notes sheet

Good morning/afternoon ladies and gentlemen. My name is

....

and I'm chairing today's debate.

The motion is ....

....

....

Speaking for the proposition today are:

....

....

....

And, on the opposition:

....

....

....

I'd now like to call on the first proposition speaker

....

to start the debate.

Thank you. Now, I'd like to call

....

to open the case for the opposition.

Thank you. Now for our second proposition speaker

....

Thank you. Before our floor debate, I'd like to invite

....

to continue the case for the opposition.

Now it's time for the floor debate. Do we have any questions from the audience? Remember, speakers won't answer straight away but will respond during their summary speeches.

Thank you for your questions. Now it is time for the summary speeches. First, I would like to call on the opposition summary speaker

....

Thank you. Now for the proposition summary speaker

....

Work with your timekeeper to count the votes.

Please raise your hands if you wish to vote for the Proposition	Now raise your hands if you agree with the Opposition	Does anyone wish to abstain?
☐	☐	☐

Either:
The motion has been carried by

☐ votes

to ☐ , with

☐ abstentions.

Or:
The motion has been defeated by

☐ votes

to ☐ , with

☐ abstentions.

© Noisy Classroom, 2017
noisyclassroom.com

the noisy classroom

3-a-side debate format
Timekeeper's notes sheet

As well as giving time signals, you can help the judges by keeping notes on timings and how many Points of Information are given and taken.

	Total time speaking	Points of Information	
		Taken	Offered to

🔔 at .... to mark the start of un-protected time (when Points of Information can be offered)

🔔 at .... to mark the end of un-protected time

🔔🔔 at .... to signal that the speech should be finishing

Speaker	Total time speaking	Taken	Offered to
1st Proposition			1st Opposition
			2nd Opposition
1st Opposition			1st Proposition
			2nd Proposition
2nd Proposition			1st Opposition
			2nd Opposition
2nd Opposition			1st Proposition
			2nd Proposition

Floor debate

🔔 at .... to signal the speech is entering its final section

🔔🔔 at .... to signal that the speech should be finishing

Speaker		Taken	Offered to
Opposition Summary			1st Proposition
			2nd Proposition
Proposition Summary			1st Opposition
			2nd Opposition

Work with the chairperson to count the votes

Proposition [ ]   Opposition [ ]   Abstentions [ ]

Appendix I: Oracy in the national curriculum

The following excerpts are taken from *The National Curriculum in England: Framework Document*.

■ The national curriculum for English aims to ensure that all pupils: Acquire a wide vocabulary, an understanding of grammar and knowledge of linguistic conventions for reading, writing and spoken language

■ Use discussion in order to learn; they should be able to elaborate and explain clearly their understanding and ideas

■ Are competent in the arts of speaking and listening, making formal presentations, demonstrating to others and participating in debate

Key Stage 3

Pupils should be taught to:

■ speak confidently and effectively, including through:

● using Standard English confidently in a range of formal and informal contexts, including classroom discussion

● giving short speeches and presentations, expressing their own ideas and keeping to the point

● participating in formal debates and structured discussions, summarising and/or building on what has been said

● improvising, rehearsing and performing play scripts and poetry in order to generate language and discuss language use and meaning, using role, intonation, tone, volume, mood, silence, stillness and action to add impact

Key Stage 4

The national curriculum for English reflects the importance of spoken language in pupils' development across the whole curriculum—cognitively, socially and linguistically. Spoken language continues to underpin the development of pupils' reading and writing during key stage 4 and teachers should therefore ensure pupils' confidence and competence in this area continue to develop. Pupils should be taught to understand and use the conventions for discussion and debate, as well as continuing to develop their skills in working collaboratively with their peers to discuss reading, writing and speech across the curriculum.

Bibliography

Books

Barton, G. (2013) *Don't Call It Literacy! What Every Teacher Needs to Know About Speaking, Listening, Reading and Writing*, Abingdon, UK: Routledge.

Burniston, C., and Parry, J. (1987) *Direct Speech*, London: Hodder and Stoughton.

Cain, S. (2012) *Quiet: The Power of Introverts in a World That Can't Stop Talking*, New York: Penguin.

Cain, S. (2016) *Quiet Power: Growing Up as an Introvert in a World That Can't Stop Talking*, New York: Penguin.

Davis, K. A., Zorwick, M. L. W., Roland, J., and Wade, M. M. (2016) *Using Debate in the Classroom: Encouraging Critical Thinking, Communication and Collaboration*, Abingdon, UK: Routledge.

English-Speaking Union (2016) *Speaking Frankly: The Case for Oracy in the Curriculum*, London: English-Speaking Union and Voice 21.

Littleton, K., and Mercer, N. (2013) *Interthinking: Putting Talk to Work*, Abingdon, UK: Routledge.

Quigley, A. (2018) *Closing the Vocabulary Gap*, Abingdon, UK: Routledge.

Ravenscroft, T. (2017) *The Missing Piece: The Essential Skills That Education Forgot*, Melton, Woodbridge, UK: John Catt.

Robinson, K., and Aronica, L. (2015) *Creative Schools*, New York: Penguin.

Robinson, M. (2013) *Trivium 21c: Preparing Young People for the Future with Lessons from the Past*, Bancyfelin, Carmarthen, UK: Crown House.

Articles, reports, blogs and papers

Akerman, R., and Neale, I. (2011) *Debating the Evidence: An International Review of Current Situation and Perceptions*, Reading, UK: CFBT Education Trust. Available at: https://issuu.com/esuorg/docs/debating-the-evidence-full-report-1.

Anderson, S., and Mezuk, B. (2012) "Participating in a policy debate program and academic achievement among at-risk adolescents in an urban public school district: 1997–2007", *Journal of Adolescence*, 35:5, pp. 1225–1235.

Argument-Centered Education, *Argument and the common core*. Available at: http://argumentcenterededucation.com/argument/argument-and-the-common-core/ (Accessed: September 2018).

Argument-Centered Education, *Research basis*. Available at: http://argumentcenterededucation.com/impact/research-basis/ (Accessed: September 2018).

Ashley, L., Duberley, J., Sommerlad, H., and Scholarios, D. (2015) *A Qualitative Evaluation of Non-educational Barriers to the Elite Professions*, London: Social Mobility and Child Poverty Commission. Available at: http://dera.ioe.ac.uk/23163/1/A_qualitative_evaluation_of_non-educational_barriers_to_the_elite_professions.pdf.

British Chamber of Commerce (2014) *Annual Workforce Survey*.

Cambridge University, *Transkills: Supporting transition to university*. Available at: https://www.transkills.admin.cam.ac.uk/skills-portal/key-skills-undergraduates (Accessed: August 2018).

CBI (2016) *The Right Combination: CBI/Pearson Education and Skills Survey 2016*, London: CBI. Available at: http://www.cbi.org.uk/cbi-prod/assets/File/pdf/cbi-education-and-skills-survey2016.pdf.

Department for Education (2014) *National Curriculum in England: Framework Document*, London: Department for Education. Available at: https://www.gov.uk/government/publications/national-curriculum-in-england-english-programmes-of-study/national-curriculum-in-england-english-programmes-of-study.

Education Endowment Foundation (2018) *Voice 21: Pilot Report and Executive Summary*, London: Education Endowment Foundation. Available at: https://educationendowmentfoundation.org.uk/public/files/Projects/Evaluation_Reports/Voice_21.pdf.

Education Endowment Foundation (2018) *Collaborative learning*. Available at: https://educationendowmentfoundation.org.uk/evidence-summaries/teaching-learning-toolkit/collaborative-learning/.

Greenland, S. (2009) "Assessing student performance in classroom debates: A valid and unbiased measurement", PhD dissertation, University of Sydney. Available at: http://debate.uvm.edu/dcpdf/greenland_HKStudy_2010.pdf.

Harrell, M., and Barbato, L. (2018) *Great managers still matter: The evolution of Google's Project Oxygen*, Rework. Available at: https://rework.withgoogle.com/blog/the-evolution-of-project-oxygen/.

Iwu, L. (2016) "Debating the education gap", TedX, London. Available at: https://www.youtube.com/watch?v=Aa5zbnl3ZQI.

Iwu, L. (May 2017) "Foreword Motion", *Dialogue*. Available at: https://www.esu.org/wp-content/uploads/2019/01/ESU_Dialogue_Spring17.pdf

McKenna, J. (2017) *Your child may need this skill as much as literacy and numeracy*, World Economic Forum. Available at: https://www.weforum.org/agenda/2017/09/oracy-literacy-skill-every-child-needs/.

Mercer, N., Dawes, L., Wegerif, R., and Sams, C. (2004) "Reasoning as a scientist: Ways of helping children to use language to learn science", *British Educational Research Journal*, 30:3, pp. 359-378.

Mercer, N., and Sams, C. (2006) "Teaching children how to use language to solve maths problems", *Language and Education*, 20:6, pp. 507-528.

Mezzo, B., Bondarenko, I., Smith, S., and Tucker, E. (2011) "Impact of participating in a policy debate program on academic achievement: Evidence from the Chicago Urban Debate League". Available at: http://urbandebate.org/Portals/0/Impact%20of%20Participatging%20in%20Policy%20Debate.pdf?ver=2016-12-19-181916-090.

Millard, W., and Menzies, L. (2016) *Oracy: The State of Speaking in Our Schools*, London: LKMco and Voice 21.

National Literacy Trust (2018) *Fake News and Critical Literacy: The Final Report of the Commission on Fake News and the Teaching of Critical Literacy in Schools*, London: National Literacy Trust. Available at: https://literacytrust.org.uk/research-services/research-reports/fake-news-and-critical-literacy-final-report/.

RCSLT (2018) *Bercow: 10 years On*. Available at: https://www.bercow10yearson.com.

Royal Bank of Canada (2018) *Humans wanted: How Canadian youth can thrive in the age of disruption*. Available at: https://www.rbc.com/dms/enterprise/futurelaunch/humans-wanted-how-canadian-youth-can-thrive-in-the-age-of-disruption.html.

Weale, S. (2018) "University drop-out rates in UK rise for third successive year", *The Guardian*, 8th March. Available at: https://www.theguardian.com/education/2018/mar/08/university-drop-out-rates-uk-rise-third-year.

Useful websites

https://www.noisyclassroom.com
https://www.upfordebate.co.uk
https://voice21.org
http://www.esu.org
http://esbuk.org
http://argumentcenterededucation.com
https://idebate.org
http://debate.uvm.edu
http://urbandebate.org

Printed in Great Britain
by Amazon